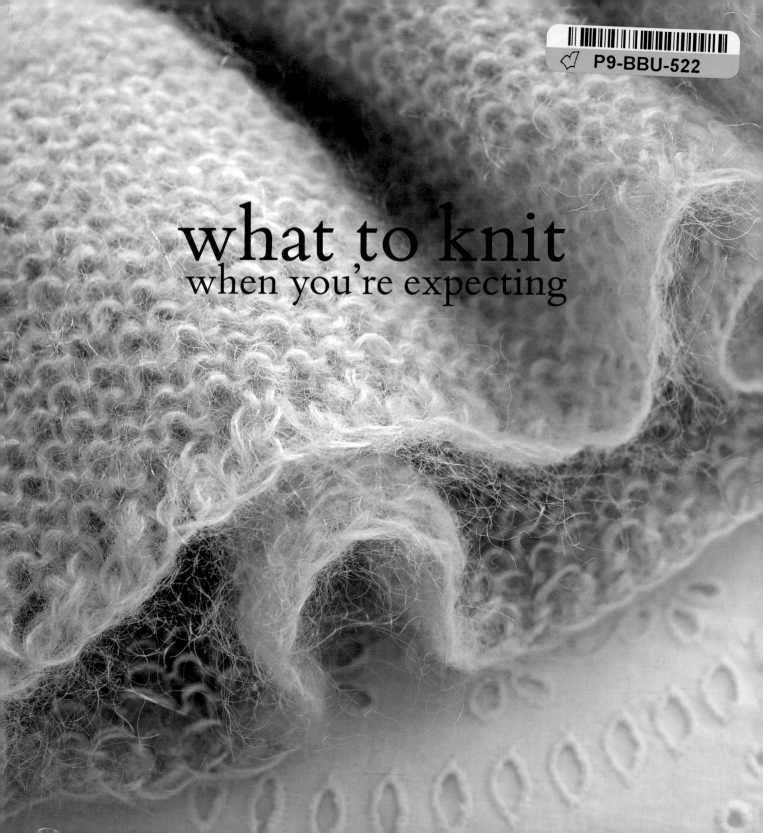

what to knit
when you're expecting

Nikki Van De Car
photography by Claire Richardson

what to knit
when you're expecting

simple
mittens,
blankets, hats
& sweaters
for baby

RUNNING PRESS
PHILADELPHIA • LONDON

First published in the United Kingdom in 2012
by Kyle Books
First published in the United States in 2012
by Running Press Book Publishers,
A Member of the Perseus Books Group

Books published by Running Press are available at
special discounts for bulk purchases in the United
States by corporations, institutions, and other
organizations. For more information, please contact
the Special Markets Department at the Perseus Books
Group, 2300 Chestnut Street, Suite 200, Philadelphia,
PA 19103, or call (800) 810-4145, ext. 5000, or e-mail
special.markets@perseusbooks.com.

ISBN 978-0-7624-4665-0
Library of Congress Control Number: 2012930288

E-book ISBN 978-0-7624-4916-3

9 8 7 6 5 4 3 2 1
Digit on the right indicates the number of this printing

Running Press Book Publishers
2300 Chestnut Street
Philadelphia, PA 19103-4371

Visit us on the web!
www.runningpress.com

To Maile

contents

introduction

My daughter Maile was born on December 16, 2009. I spent the months before her birth knitting constantly to keep my hands busy, and to help the time before her arrival pass more quickly, and to reassure myself that everything was going to be all right during my very difficult pregnancy. I knitted sweaters, blankets, burp cloths, and stuffed animals. And I put my hopes and my love for my child into every stitch.

Every pattern in this book has a story. And while I confess that I did not knit 30 patterns in nine months, I did knit many of these for Maile, and the others were knit over the years for those friends whose lives have touched ours.

In the course of Maile's first year, I learned which knitted items are useful, and which ones are, shall we say, merely decorative – those that sat in her drawer, never to be worn. I've included only the best and most useful projects in this book. The patterns are all relatively simple, so that they can be knit while your mind is elsewhere, and they are all practical: they can actually be worn, used or played with.

This book is organized by trimester: the ten patterns in the chapter The First Trimester are slightly more difficult as, during this trimester, your mind is still likely to be relatively clear, and you probably have plenty of time to finish a longer project, such as a baby blanket or a more complex hooded jacket. The Second Trimester focuses on patterns specific to gender, for those of us who choose to find out ahead of time. They are also at the intermediate level, but are on the faster side, as time grows short during this phase of pregnancy. The patterns in The Third Trimester are strictly easy and short because, by now, that "pregnancy brain" is likely to have kicked in, and you are both distracted and impatient.

What To Knit When You're Expecting is intended to satisfy, in part at least, that nesting instinct that can only be fully sated by creating things yourself. Whether it's painting the nursery, putting together the crib by yourself (not recommended), or knitting an entire wardrobe for your baby, a pregnant woman's needs must be honored.

tips & techniques

Sizing information

It is an understatement to say that babies vary widely in size. A six-month-old baby can outweigh a one-year-old, and a newborn is smaller than we can imagine. These measurements are for your "average" baby, and the garments in this book vary in terms of positive or negative ease. Ease is the roominess of the fit, so positive ease means a slightly baggier garment (like the Hannah Jacket) and negative ease means a tighter garment (like the bodice of the Emily Dress). If you're not sure which size to make, knit the larger size – it will fit eventually.

A note on yarns

You won't find much acrylic here. And while I know some of my suggestions are a little extravagant (cashmere? For a baby?), I have found that wool, cotton and, yes, even cashmere, are perfectly practical.

For many people, it is the washing instructions that come with pure wool, cashmere and cotton, that are off-putting, but it's not difficult if you use your head. I do all Maile's wash as one load, using a mild baby detergent such as Dreft. I toss the knitted items in with everything else and run it all on the delicate cycle. I lay out the knitted items flat to dry, and that's it! Washing requires no more work than garments made using acrylic yarns, and I get the pleasure of feeling something nearly as soft as Maile's skin when I hold her.

	0–3 months	3–6 months	6–12 months
weight	5–10lbs	8–12lbs	12–18lbs
height	22–26 in	26–30 in	30–33.5 in
chest circumference	17.5 in	18 in	19 in
head circumference	15 in	15.75 in	17 in
sleeve length (from underarm to wrist)	6 in	6.5 in	7 in
hip circumference (with diaper on)	19 in	20 in	21 in
inseam	6.5 in	7.5 in	8.5 in

Abbreviations

CC contrast color

CO cast on (using the long-tail cast-on technique, unless otherwise specified)

dpns double-pointed needles

k knit

k1tbl knit 1 stitch through the back of the loop

k2tog knit 2 stitches together (to decrease the number of stitches by 1)

kf&b knit front and back – knit into the front and back of the stitch (to increase the number of stitches by 1)

m1 make one stitch – using your left needle, pick up the bar between the stitch on your left needle and the stitch on your right needle. Knit this new stitch (to increase the number of stitches by 1)

m1p make 1 stitch purlwise – using your left needle, pick up the bar between the stitch on your left needle and the stitch on your right needle. Purl this stitch (to increase the number of stitches by 1)

MC main color

p purl

p2tog purl 2 stitches together (to decrease the number of stitches by 1)

p2togtbl purl 2 stitches together through the back of the loop (to decrease the number of stitches by 1)

pm place marker

pf&b purl front and back – purl into the front and back of the stitch (to increase the number of stitches by 1)

RS right side of the work

sl slip – slip the stitch or marker (as instructed) onto the right needle

sl 1 k1 psso slip 1, knit 1, pass the stitch over – slip 1 stitch purlwise, knit the next stitch, then pass the slipped stitch over the knitted stitch (to decrease the number of stitches by 1)

sl 1 k2tog psso slip 1 stitch purlwise, knit 2 stitches together, pass the slipped stitch over the new knit stitch (to decrease the number of stitches by 2)

sl sl k slip, slip, knit – slip next 2 stiches knitwise. Slip the tip of the left needle into the front of the slipped stitches and knit them together (to decrease the number of stitches by 1)

st stitch

sts stitches

st st stockinette stitch

WS wrong side of the work

x times (as in, repeat 3 times)

yb yarn back – bring the working yarn to the back of the knitting

yf yarn forwards – bring the working yarn to the front of the knitting

( ) repeat the instructions inside parentheses as many times as is indicated, for example (kf&b) × 2

* repeat the instructions following/between asterisks as indicated

Techniques

Casting On Stitches

There is a variety of cast-on methods you can use, each with its own benefits. The methods below are used in the patterns in this book.

Long-tail cast-on method (A)

Most of the patterns in this book use long-tail cast-on. If the pattern doesn't specify a cast-on technique, long-tail is the one I had in mind, but feel free to use whichever method you like best.

Pull out a strand of yarn approximately three times the length of your first row. Err on the longer side to avoid having to cast on twice. Make a slipknot here, then insert your needle into the loop. *Holding the needle in your right hand, loop one strand of yarn around your left thumb, and the other strand around your left index finger. Keep your fingers stretched out, as shown. Slip the needle into the front of the loop around your thumb, and into the back of the loop around your index finger, then drop the thumb loop onto the needle. Pull tight. Repeat from * until you have cast on enough stitches.

Provisional cast-on method (B)

Using a crochet hook, chain four stitches more than need to be cast on. Break the yarn, and knot the chain. Turn it over to the wrong side, and insert your left knitting needle into the first or second loop on the underside of the chain. Knit this stitch onto your right needle, and repeat until you have picked up, and knit the number of stitches you need to cast on.

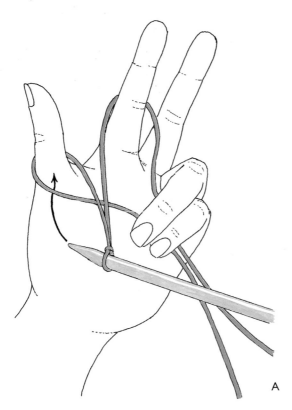

A

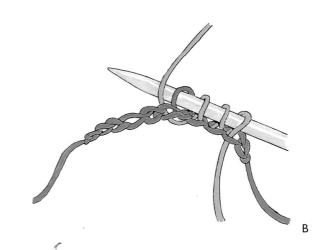

B

C

Backward-loop cast-on method (C)

Place your left index finger behind the yarn, and wind it around your finger. Insert the tip of the right needle into the loop. Remove your finger and pull tight. Repeat until you have cast on enough stitches.

Cable cast-on method (D)

Make a slipknot, and place it on the left needle. Knit this stitch, and drop the new stitch onto the left needle. *Insert your right needle in the space between the two stitches, and knit a stitch from this space. Drop your new stitch onto the left needle. Repeat from * using the space between the first two stitches on the left needle to cast on from until you have cast on enough stitches.

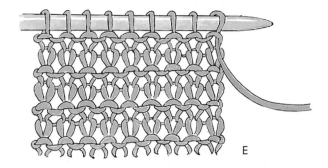

E

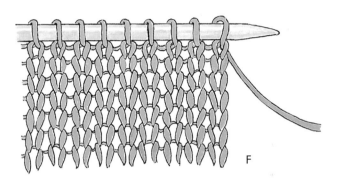

F

D

Garter stitch (E)

When working in rows, knit all stitches, both right side, and wrong side. When working in the round, alternate knit and purl rounds.

Stockinette stitch (F)

When working in rows, alternate knit and purl rows. When working in the round, knit all stitches.

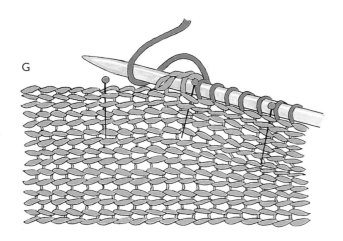

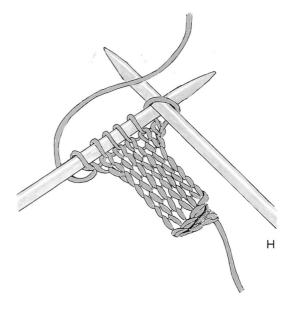

Picking up stitches (G)

When picking up stitches along the cast-on or cast-off edge, with right side facing, insert your left needle into the "V" at the top of the row just inside the edge. Knit this stitch onto your right needle, and repeat until you have picked up enough stitches. When picking up stitches along the side edge, turn your work sideways (C). With the right side facing, and working between the first and second columns of stitches in from that edge, insert a needle between the bars between two stitches. Loop the working yarn over the needle and draw the loop through the stitch to form a stitch on the needle. Repeat until you have picked up enough stitches.

I-cord (H)

These instructions are for a 6-stitch i-cord. Using a double-pointed needle, cast on 6 stitches. Knit these stitches, then slide them to the opposite end of the right needle. Bring the working yarn around the back of the needle, pull it tight, then, instead of turning the needle, transfer it to your left hand, and knit 6 from the opposite end of the needle. Slide the stitches down to the other end of the needle, and repeat. Do not turn the needle at any stage, and continue working in this way until your i-cord is as long as desired.

Magic loop knitting (I)

Magic loop is a technique that allows you to work in the round on a small number of stitches on a set of long circular needles with a flexible wire rather than double-pointed needles. Some people prefer the technique to using double-pointed needles. None of the patterns here require an understanding of magic loop knitting, but the technique can be helpful.

Once you have cast on, slide your stitches to the centre of the flexible wire. Divide them in half, then, at the half-way point, pull the wire out between them into a loop. Slide the left first of the stitches onto your left needle, and adjust the wire as necessary to allow the second group of stitches to rest on the wire. Bend the wire as necessary so that your right needle is free to work. Knit across the stitches on your left needle, then transfer these stitches from the right needle onto the wire. Now slide the resting stitches onto your left needle. Repeat to work in the round. Ensure that, each time you change from working one set of stitches to the next, you pull the working yarn tight to avoid the appearance of ladders between sets of stitches.

Knitting in the round

All the sleeves and pant legs in this book have been written to be seamed – the pieces are sewn together after knitting. Personally, I find seaming is easier than knitting in the round, and makes for a neat, sturdy finished garment. However, not everyone likes seaming. Many savvy and dpn-loving knitters will want to work the sleeves in the round. If you want to do so, you may want to decrease the stitch count by a stitch or two, since the patterns are written to allow for a couple of stitches to be used for seaming. Also bear in mind that joining pant legs that have been knitted in the round is a tricky (but not impossible!) business.

Finishing

How you finish off your garment makes all the difference to the completed piece. There are a variety of methods you can use to cast off your stitches, and to sew your knitted pieces together, each with its own advantages. Make sure you block your knitted pieces before sewing them together (see page 17).

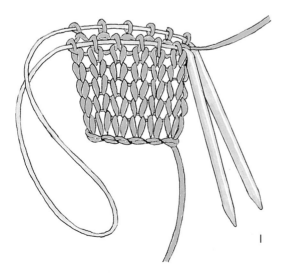

I

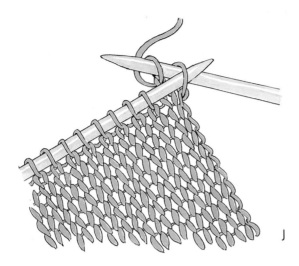

J

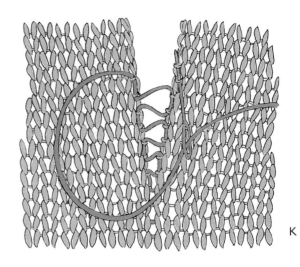

K

Casting off (J)

Casting off begins by knitting two stitches. Then, *insert your left needle into the first stitch on your right needle that you knitted (the stitch that does not have a strand of yarn hanging from it), and pass this stitch over the second stitch, and over the tip of your right needle. One stitch remains on your right needle. Knit one stitch from the left needle. Repeat from * until there are no stitches on your left needle, and only one stitch remains on your right needle. Break the yarn, and draw it through this remaining stitch. Pull tight.

There is a trick to keep this edge nice and stretchy: use a needle one size larger than the size you've been knitting with as your right needle. This isn't necessary, as long as you don't pull too tight with the working yarn, but it does make things a little easier.

Mattress stitch (K)

This is a fantastic seaming stitch; it's easy enough to do, and creates a strong, flat, and nearly invisible seam. Lay your two pieces of work flat with the right sides facing you, with the two edges that are to be joined parallel. Thread a tapestry needle with a length of yarn, and insert the needle into the first row of stitches on the edge to the left, placing the needle underneath the bar between the first and second stitches in from the edge. Pull through, then place the needle under the matching bar between the first and second row of stitches in on the right edge.

*Now insert your needle between the first and second stitches in from the left edge again, and place the needle under the bars of the next two rows, thereby pulling the yarn under two bars at a time, instead of just one. Repeat on the right edge from *, working back and forth, sewing two rows at a time until the entire length is sewn. Remember to keep working between the first and second stitches in from the edge.

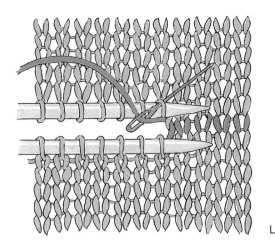

L

Kitchener stitch (L)

Kitchener stitch works by grafting two equal-numbered sets of live stitches together by mimicking the way the yarn moves as it creates a knit stitch, making it appear as if there is no seam at all.

Hold two needles with the equal-numbered sets of stitches that are to be grafted together parallel, with their right sides both facing out, and the working yarn attached to the back set of stitches. Before you can begin grafting the stitches, you must prepare them for grafting. Thread your yarn through a tapestry needle, and insert the needle through the first stitch on the first knitting needle downwards, as if to purl. Pull the needle through the stitch, but leave the stitch on the knitting needle. Draw the yarn under the first knitting needle and insert your tapestry needle up through the first stitch on the second needle as if to knit. Again, leave this stitch on the knitting needle.

Now you are ready to graft the two sets of stitches together. *Insert your tapestry needle through the first stitch on the first needle upwards, as if to knit, pull the yarn through, then pull the stitch off of the knitting needle. Now insert your tapestry needle through the next stitch on the first needle downwards as if to purl, and pull the yarn through. Leave this stitch on the knitting needle. Insert your tapestry needle through the first stitch on the second needle downwards as if to purl, and pull the stitch off of the knitting needle as you pull the yarn through. Insert your tapestry needle through the next stitch on the second needle upwards as if to knit, and pull the yarn through. Leave this stitch on the knitting needle.

Repeat from * until all the stitches have been pulled off the needles.

Blocking

My favorite method of blocking is quite aggressive, and requires by far the least effort. Dunk your knitted item into a sink full of lukewarm water and swish it around a bit until you're sure it's soaked through. Very gently squeeze out most of the excess water – you don't want to wring it, but you don't need to leave it sopping wet, either. Then spread it out flat on a surface you won't need for a while, stretching it out to the dimensions you want it to have (but be careful not to overstretch – the garment will tell you how big it wants to be). Let it dry completely, flipping it over if you need to.

You can simply repeat this lay-flat-to-dry process with your knitted items when you've washed them after they've been worn, but be sure to pay attention to the instructions on the yarn label.

the first trimester

For me, despite not knowing I was in it for the first month and a half, the first trimester dragged—and so I knitted like crazy. Beginner knitters may want to try the simpler summer sky blanket, while the more adventurous may want to explore the honeycomb.

summer sky blanket

This airy cotton blanket is very quick knitting. You start with a large stockinette rectangular sky, then pick up an edging of fluffy clouds.

SIZE
Approximately 28 x 30 in (71 x 76 cm)

MATERIALS
3 x 3½oz skeins Blue Sky Alpacas Worsted Cotton
   (shade: 628 Azul) for MC
2 x 3½oz skeins Blue Sky Alpacas Worsted Cotton
   (shade: 614 Drift) for CC
1 x set of US 9 circular needles
Tapestry needle

GAUGE
15 sts and 23 rows to 4 in (10 cm) over st st using
   US 9 needles.

Rice stitch

Row 1 (WS): k all sts.

Row 2 (RS): p1, *k1tbl, p1, repeat from * to end.

Pattern

Using MC, CO 96 sts.

Work in st st until piece measures 28 in (72 cm), ending with a WS row.

Cast off all sts. Weave in ends.

EDGING

Using CC, with RS facing, pick up and k 97 sts along cast off edge. Work in rice stitch for a total of 11 rows ending with a WS row. Cast off all but the last st.

Leaving this st on your needle, turn blanket counter-clockwise, and pick up and k 6 sts along the rice-stitch edging. Then pick up and k 98 sts along the long edge of the blanket. 105 sts.

Work in rice stitch for 11 rows ending with a WS row. Cast off all but the last st.

Leaving this st on your needle, turn blanket counter-clockwise again, and pick up and k 6 sts along the rice-stitch edge. Now pick up and k 96 sts along the CO edge of blanket. 103 sts.

Work in rice stitch for 11 rows ending with a WS row. Cast off all but the last st.

Leaving this st on your needle, turn blanket counter-clockwise again, and pick up and k 6 sts along the rice-stitch edge. Pick up and k 98 sts along the right edge of blanket, then pick up and k 6 sts along final rice-stitch edge to complete the rectangle. 111 sts.

Work in rice stitch for 11 rows ending with a WS row. Cast off all sts (including the last st).

Finishing

Weave in ends and block as desired.

Noah sweater

Named for my stepson, this is a classic sweater for a classic little kid. The cotton yarn and keyhole opening make it cool enough for sunny yet breezy days.

SIZES 0–3 (3–6, 6–12 months) (shown in 0–3 months).

MATERIALS
2 x 1¾ oz balls Amy Butler Belle Organic DK (shade: 013 Moonflower) for MC
1 (2, 2) x 1¾ oz balls Amy Butler Belle Organic DK (shade: 017 Zinc) for CC
1 x set of US 5 knitting needles
Tapestry needle
1 x 11.5 mm button
Needle and thread

GAUGE
23 sts and 33 rows to 4 in (10 cm) over st st using US 5 needles.

Pattern

BACK/FRONT (MAKE 2)

Using MC, CO 50 (54, 58) sts.

Work in garter stitch for 6 rows.

Work in st st stitch until piece measures 6 in/16 cm (7 in/18 cm, 8 in/20 cm), ending with a WS row. Piece measures 9 in/23 cm (10.25 in/26 cm, 11.5 in/29.5 cm).

Cast off 2 sts at the beginning of the next 2 rows. 46 (50, 54) sts.

Next row: k2, sl sl k, k to last 4 sts, k2tog, k2. 44 (48, 52) sts.

*Next row: p to end.

Next row: k2, sl sl k, k to last 4 sts, k2tog, k2. 42 (46, 50) sts.

Repeat from * until 24 sts remain.

Next row: p to end.

Cast off all sts.

SLEEVES (MAKE 2)

Using CC, CO 26 (28, 32) sts.

Work in garter stitch for 5 rows.

**Work in st st for 7 rows, starting with a p row.

Next row (RS): k2, m1, k to last 2 sts, m1, k2. 28 (30, 34) sts.

Repeat from ** until there are 36 (40, 44) sts, then work even until piece measures 6 in/15 cm (6½ in/17 cm, 7½/19 cm), ending with a WS row. Piece measures 8.75 in/22 cm (10 in/25 cm, 11 in/28.5 cm).

Cast off 2 sts at the beginning of the next two rows. 32 (36, 40) sts.

Next row: k2, sl sl k, k to last 4 sts, k2tog, k2. 30 (34, 38) sts.

****Next row:* p to end.

Next row: k2, sl sl k, k to last 4 sts, k2tog, k2. 28 (32, 36) sts.

Repeat from *** 9 (11, 13) times more. 10 sts.

Next row: p to end.

Cast off all sts.

POCKET

Using CC, CO 20 (22, 24) sts.

Beginning with a k row, work in st st for 20 (22, 24) rows.

P 2 rows.

Cast off purlwise.

Finishing

Sew front and back side seams together up to underarm raglan edge. Set sleeves into front and back pieces along raglan edge and join using MC on all but the front right raglan edge. For this, sew 1¼ in (3 cm) up from armpit, and leave the rest of the seam unsewn. Sew sleeve seams using CC. Sew on pocket as pictured. Weave in ends.

NECKBAND

Using CC, with RS facing, pick up and k 60 sts around neckline. Do not join.

Next row: k to end.

Next row: k1, yf, k2tog, k to end.

Cast off all sts.

Sew button opposite buttonhole.

simple mittens

These mittens are for slightly warmer weather—they're light, and the thumbs allow for gripping toys, gesturing at passing dogs and cars, and squeezing your hand.

SIZE 0–12 months

MATERIALS
1 x 1¾ oz ball Debbie Bliss Cashmerino Aran
   (shade: 202 Light Blue)
1 x set of US 8 double-pointed needles
Spare yarn or stitch holder
Tapestry needle
½ in-wide (1.5 cm) elastic
Needle and thread
Stitch marker

GAUGE
21 sts and 28 rows to 4 in (10 cm) over st st
   using US 8 needles.

PREPARE ELASTIC

Cut a 5½ in-length (14 cm) of elastic. Fold into a circle with a ¾ in (2 cm) overlap. Using the needle and thread, stitch down the overlap.

Pattern (make 2)

CUFF

CO 26 sts. Divide sts evenly around dpns, and join to work in the round.

Round 1: *k1, p1, repeat from * until end of round.

Repeat this round until piece measures 2⅓ in (6 cm). This will form the cuff.

FIT ELASTIC

Push the cuff up through your needles so that it is poking out of the top of the knitted tube with the WS facing. Place elastic around the cuff against the WS, ⅔ in (1.5 cm) below the CO edge. Now fold the CO edge over the elastic to encase it within the knitting. Using your left needle, pick up the first st from the CO edge, and k it together with the first st on your left needle, effectively sewing the elastic into the mitten. Pick up the second st from the CO edge, and k it together with the second st on your needle. Continue in this way until you've reached the end of the round, and the elastic is encased within the cuff. Now push the cuff back inside the needles so that the RS is facing. If this process seems intimidating, you can always sew the elastic in after you finish knitting. Instructions are given in the pattern for Cuffed Pants (see page 80). But this knitting-in method is easier than it sounds.

THUMB GUSSET

Next round: k to end.

Next round: k2, m1, k to 1 st before end of round, m1, k1. 28 sts.

K 2 rounds.

Next round: k3, m1, k to 2 sts before end of round, m1, k2. 30 sts.

Next round: k to end.

Next round: K to 3 sts before end of round, place next 7 sts on spare yarn or stitch holder. CO 1 st using the backward-loop CO method (see page 13), and place a stitch marker on this st to denote the end of the round. CO 2 sts then k to the end of the round. 26 sts.

BODY OF MITTEN

K until st st section measures 2¾ in.

Next round: k1, sl sl k, k7, k2tog, k2, sl sl k, k7, k2tog, k1. 22 sts.

Next round: k to end.

Next round: k1, sl sl k, k5, k2tog, k2, sl sl k, k5, k2tog, k1. 18 sts.

Next round: k to end.

Next round: k1, sl sl k, k3, k2tog, k2, sl sl k, k3, k2tog, k1. 14 sts.

Next round: k to end.

Place first 7 sts onto one dpn, and second 7 sts onto another. Graft top of mitten together using Kitchener stitch (see page 17).

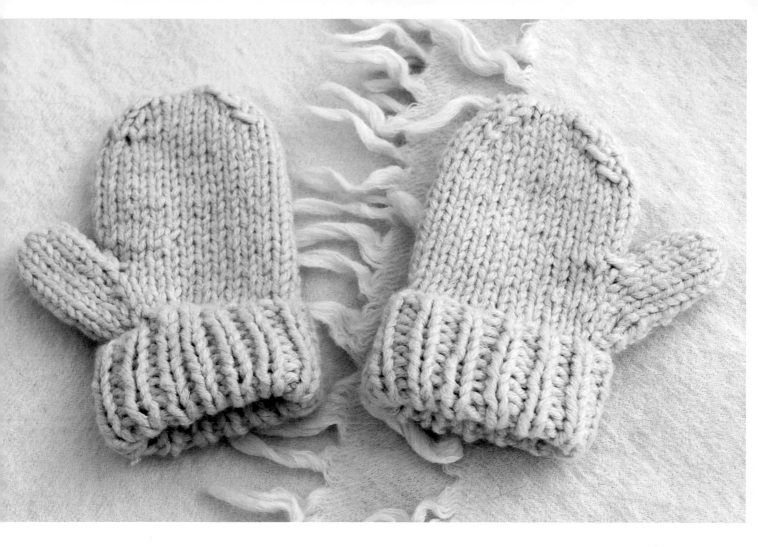

THUMB

Place the 7 thumb sts onto 2 dpns.

Next row: k7, pick up 5 sts as follows: 1 st at break of thumb and mitten, 3 sts from the 3 CO sts, and 1 st at break of thumb and mitten. 12 sts.

K 7 rounds.

Finishing

Break yarn leaving a long tail. Draw tail through remaining sts, and pull tight.

Weave in ends.

thrummed mittens

Thrums are small pieces of fleecy unspun
fiber that you knit into your work to create
a pattern on the right side, and a warm,
fleecy wrong side. These thrummed mittens
are quick and easy to make, and have no
thumbholes—your baby's full hand will be
encased in the wonderfully warm, fleecy
interior. If you don't have easy access
to unspun fibers (known as wool tops), a
loosely spun bulky yarn will do.

SIZE 0–12 months

MATERIALS
1 x 1¾ oz ball Rowan Kid Classic
    (shade: 828 Feather)
1 oz unspun fiber
US 9 double pointed needles
½ in-wide (1.5 cm) piece of elastic
Tapestry needle
Needle and thread

GAUGE
20 sts and 27 rows to 4 in (10 cm) over st st
    using US 9 needles.

Note: Placing thrums

To knit a thrum into your work, insert the right needle into the st as normal, then wrap a thrum around the right needle. Now wrap the yarn around the right needle, as normal, then k both yarn and thrum together as one st.

PREPARE THRUMS

Cut or tear fiber or yarn into small pieces that are approximately 3 in (8 cm) in length, and twist the until they are ½ in (0.5 cm) in width. You'll need 80 thrums.

PREPARE ELASTIC

Cut a 5½ in-length (14 cm) of elastic. Fold into a circle with a 1 in (2 cm) overlap. Using the needle and thread, stitch down the overlap.

Abbreviations

thrum 1: place thrum in next st

Pattern (make 2)

CUFF

CO 24 sts. Divide sts evenly around dpns, and join to knit in the round. Place marker to mark end of round.

First round: *k 1, p1, repeat from * until end of round.

Repeat this round until piece measures 2½ in (6 cm). This will form the cuff.

FIT ELASTIC

Push the cuff up through your needles so that it is poking out of the top of the knitted tube with the WS facing. Place elastic around the cuff against the WS, 1 in (1.5 cm) below the CO edge. Now fold the CO edge over the elastic to encase it within the knitting. Using your left needle, pick up the first st from the CO edge, and k it together with the first st on your left needle, effectively sewing the elastic into the mitten. Pick up the second st from the CO edge, and k it together with the second st on your needle. Continue in this way until you've reached the end of the round, and the elastic is encased within the cuff. Now push the cuff back inside the needles so that the RS is facing. (If this process seems intimidating, you can always sew the elastic in after you finish knitting. Instructions are given in the pattern for Cuffed Pants (see page 80). But it is easier than it sounds).

BODY OF MITTEN

First round: kf&b, k10, (kf&b) × 2, k10, kf&b. 28 sts.

Next round: k to end.

Next round: kf&b, k12, (kf&b) × 2, k12, kf&b. 32 sts.

Next round: k to end.

Thrum round: *k3, thrum 1. Repeat from * to end of round.

k3 rounds.

Repeat last 4 rounds twice.

Next round: Work thrum round once more.

Next round: k1, sl sl k, k10, k2tog, k2, sl sl k, k10, k2tog, k1. 28 sts.

Next round: k to end.

Next round: k1, sl sl k, k8, k2tog, k2, sl sl k, k8, k2tog, k1. 24 sts.

Next round: k1, thrum 1, (k3, thrum 1) × 2, (k1, thrum 1) × 2, (k3, thrum 1) × 2, k1, thrum 1.

Next round: k1, sl sl k, k6, k2tog, k2, sl sl k, k6, k2tog, k1. 20 sts.

Next round: k to end.

Place first 10 sts onto one dpn, and second 10 sts onto another. Graft top of mitten together using Kitchener stitch (see page 17).

Finishing
Weave in ends if desired, mittens can be sewn to ends of a length of ribbon.

leg warmers

My daughter Maile hates having her diaper changed, and her kicking feet always make it impossible to get her pants on and off. Legwarmers are an elegant solution to this problem, and show off those delicious thighs as well! These legwarmers are worked from the top down, and have a pull-tab and button so they'll stay up without cutting off circulation.

SIZES 0–3 (3–6, 6–12) months. (Shown in 6–12 months)

MATERIALS
1 skein Madelinetosh Tosh Merino Light
    (shade: Tern), a single-ply fingering weight yarn
1 set of US 2 double-pointed needles
3 × stitch markers
Tapestry needle
2 × 8 mm buttons
Needle and thread

GAUGE
30 sts and 38.5 rows to 4 in (10 cm) over st st
    using US 2 needles.

Turn leaf lace pattern (worked over 23 sts)

Round 1: k8, k2tog, yf, k1, p1, k1, yf, sl 1 k1 psso, k8

Round 2: k7, k2tog, k2, yf, p1, keep yf, k2, sl 1 k1 psso, k7

Round 3: k6, k2tog, k1, yf, k2, p1, k2, yf, k1, sl 1 k1 psso, k6

Round 4: k5, k2tog, k3, yf, k1, p1, k1, yf, k3, sl 1 k1 psso, k5

Round 5: k4, k2tog, k2, yf, k3, p1, k3, yf, k2, sl 1 k1 psso, k4

Round 6: k3, k2tog, k4, yf, k2, p1, k2, yf, k4, sl 1 k1 psso, k3

Round 7: k2, k2tog, k3, yf, k4, p1, k4, yf, k3, sl 1 k1 psso, k2

Round 8: k1, k2tog, k5, yf, k3, p1, k3, yf, k5, sl 1 k1 psso, k1

Round 9: k2tog, k4, yf, k5, p1, k5, yf, k4, sl 1 k1 psso

Round 10: k11, p1, k11

Round 11: same as r10.

Round 12: same as r10.

Linen stitch

Row 1: *p1, yb, sl 1 purlwise, yf, repeat from * to last st, k1.

Row 2: *sl 1 purlwise, yb, k1, yf, repeat from * to last st, sl 1.

Pattern (make 2)

CO 44 (48, 52) sts, divide sts evenly onto dpns and join to work in the round. Place marker to mark the end of the round.

Round 1: *k1, p1, repeat from * to end of round.

Repeat round 1 until piece measures 1 in (3 cm).

Next round: k10 (12, 14), pm, work next 23 sts as row 1 of turn leaf lace pattern, pm, k to end.

(Note: The turn leaf lace pattern is off-center. Don't worry – this won't show in the finished legwarmers.)

***Next round:* k to marker, work row 2 of turn leaf lace pattern, k to end.

Continue to work in turn leaf lace pattern as set for 1 in/2.5 cm (1¼ in/3 cm, 1½ in/4 cm).

Decrease round: k1, k2tog, k to marker, work next row of turn leaf lace pattern, k to 4 sts before end of round, sl 1 k1 psso, k2.

Repeat from ** 3 times. 36 (40, 44) sts.

Continue to k each round, keeping to turn leaf lace pattern as set, until piece measures 5 in/13 cm (6 in/15 cm, 7 in/19 cm) from CO edge.

Next round: *k1, p1, repeat from * to end of round.

Continue in rib for 1 in (3 cm).

Cast off all sts.

TABS

LEFT LEGWARMER

Mark a st 3 rows down and 5 sts to the right of the top center back. Turn legwarmer sideways so that the ankle cuff is to your right and pick up 7 sts in a straight line down along cuff from the marker.

Work in linen stitch for 1½ in (4 cm), ending with row 1. Note: linen stitch does seem a bit tricky at first glance, but it's easy enough once you get the hang of it, and it doesn't stretch at all, which is useful here. If you'd rather knit the tabs in garter stitch, work only ¾ in (2 cm), since garter stitch does stretch.

Buttonhole row: (RS) sl 1, yb, k1, yf, sl 1, yb, k2tog, yf, k1, yf, sl 1.

Next row: p1, yb, sl 1, yf, p3, yb, sl 1, p1.

Last row: *yf, sl 1, k1, repeat from * to last st, yf, sl 1.

Cast off all sts.

RIGHT LEGWARMER

Work as for left legwarmer, this time turning the legwarmer sideways so that the ankle cuff is to your left to pick up sts.

Cast off all sts.

Finishing

Place button so that the tab pulls slightly, helping to hold up the legwarmer. If possible, you may want to have the baby you're knitting for try them on so you can place the button in the ideal spot. Either way, the button can be moved to accommodate growing bodies. Repeat with other legwarmer.

Weave in ends. Block as desired.

Hannah jacket

My stepdaughter Hannah had a fleece jacket like this one when she was little. I didn't know her then, but there is a photo of her that I love, in which she is crouching down in the middle of a stone path to pick up a tiny red fall leaf. She looks like a wood elf.

SIZES 0–3 (3–6, 6–12) months (shown in 3–6 months)

MATERIALS
2 x 3½ oz skeins Spud and Chloe Sweater
   (shade: 7516 Grape Jelly) for MC
1 x 3½ oz skein Spud and Chloe Sweater
   (shade: 7507 Moonlight) for CC
1 x set of US 9 16 in circular needles
1 x set of US 8 16 in circular needles
1 x set of US 8 double-pointed needles
1 x crochet hook
Tapestry needle and needle and thread.
3 x small wooden toggles
4 x stitch markers
Small amount of mercerized cotton yarn in a CC

GAUGE
17 sts and 26 rows to 4 in (10 cm) over st st
using US 8 needles.

Pattern

YOKE

Using US 9 needles, MC and the mercerized cotton yarn, CO 24 (28, 32) sts using the provisional cast-on method (see page 12).

Row 1 (WS): k1, p3 (4, 5), pm, p 4, pm, p 8 (10, 12), pm, p 4, pm, p to last st, k1.

Raglan row: p1, *k to 1 st before marker, m1, k1, sl marker, k1, m1, repeat from * 3 more times, k to last st, p1.

***Next row:* k1, p to last st, k1.

Next row: repeat raglan row.

Repeat from ** until there are 128 (140, 152) sts.

Next row (WS): k1, p to last st, k1.

Next row (RS): p 1, k to first marker, remove marker, place next 30 (32, 34) sts on spare cotton yarn for left sleeve, CO 2 sts using the backward-loop cast-on method (see page 13), k to next marker, remove marker place next 30 (32, 34) sts on spare cotton yarn for right sleeve, remove marker CO 2 sts using the backward-loop cast-on method, k to last st, p1. 72 (80, 88) sts.

BODY

Work 5 rows as set.

Next row (RS): p1, k 16 (18, 20), m1, k1, pm, k1, m1, k 34 (38, 42), m1, k1, pm, k1, m1, k 16 (18, 20), p1. 76 (84, 92) sts.

***Work 5 rows even as established.

Next row (RS): p1, (k to 1 st before marker, m1, k1, sl marker, k1, m1) x 2, k to last st, p1.

Repeat from * 2 (3, 4) times more. 88 (100, 112) sts.

Work 5 rows as set.

Next row (RS): k 1 row.

Piece measures 8.5 in/21.5 cm (9.5 in/23.5 cm, 11 in/ 26.5 cm). Cast off all sts knitwise.

SLEEVES

Place right sleeve sts on needle.

Row 1 (RS): cast off 1 st, k to end.

Row 2 (WS): cast off 1 st, p to end (28 (30, 32) sts.

*Work 10 (11, 12) rows.

Next row (RS): decrease 1 st at each end. (For RS decreases, k1, sl sl k, k to last 3 sts, k2tog, k1. For WS decreases, p1, p2tog, p to last 3 sts, p2togtbl, p1.)

Repeat from * until 24 (26, 28) sts remain. Work even until sleeve measures 8.5 in/22 cm (9.25 in/23.5 cm, 10.5 in/26.5 in) from cast-on edge.

Next row (RS): k 1 row.

Next row (WS): cast off all sts.

Repeat with left sleeve.

HOOD

Carefully unravel provisional CO by undoing the crochet chain and pulling free one st at a time. Place each neckline st on needles.

With RS facing, attach yarn.

Next row: p1, m1, k4 (6, 8), m1, k7, m1, k7, m1, k4 (6, 8), m1, p1. 29 (33, 37) sts.

Next row: k1, p to last st, k1.

Next row: p1, m1, k5 (7, 9), m1, k8, m1, k8, m1, k6 (8, 10), m1, p1. 34 (38, 42) sts.

*Next row: k1, p to last st, k1.

Next row: p1, k to last st, p1.

Repeat from * until hood measures 6½ in/16 cm (7 in/18 cm, 8 in/20 cm), ending with a WS row.

Next row: k17 (19, 21) sts, then turn. Hold your needles parallel and graft the two sets of sts together using Kitchener stitch (see page 17).

Finishing

Weave in ends and sew sleeve seams.

SLEEVE EDGING

With RS facing, and using dpns and CC, beginning at seam, pick up and k 24 (26, 28) sts around cast-off edge of sleeve cuff. Join to work in the round. K 1 round.

CO 3 sts using cable cast-on method (see page 13).

Next round: *k2, p2tog, sl sts from right needle to left needle, pulling yarn around and across back of sts, repeat from * around.

Break yarn, leaving a long tail. Draw through remaining 4 sts. Sew edge of i-cord together.

Repeat with second sleeve.

BODY EDGING

Starting at center lower back, using CC and US 8 circular needles, pick up and k 44 (50, 58) sts across right side of back 38 (44, 50) sts from right front, then 36 (38, 40) sts around hood, 38 (44, 50) sts around left front, and 44 (50, 58) sts across left back to center back. Join to work in the round. (If you find it easier, you could instead pick up 1 st for each st across bottom back, and 2 sts for every 3 rows up right front, around hood and down left front.)

Next round: k to end.

CO 3 sts onto left needle using cable cast-on method (see page 13).

Next round: *k2, p2tog, sl sts from right needle to left needle, pulling yarn around and across back of sts, repeat from * to end.

Break yarn, leaving a long tail. Draw through remaining 4 sts. Sew edge of i-cord together.

Weave in ends.

TOGGLES AND TIES

Attach CC yarn and using crochet hook, chain 3⅕ in (8 cm) and sew loop onto sweater as pictured. Repeat until you have 3 loops. Attach toggles opposite loops.

honeycomb blanket

I knit this versatile blanket of concentric squishy squares for my baby, but it spends just as much time on various adult laps as it does wrapped around her. Comforting and cozy, this simple pattern knits up very quickly, and while it does look homey, it has a lovely modern look, too. Worked in stockinette stitch, garter stitch, and an hourglass-looking honeycomb stitch, the pattern changes just often enough to keep things interesting.

SIZE Approximately 32 × 32 in (80 × 80 cm)

MATERIALS
4 × 3½ oz skeins Malabrigo Worsted
   (shade: 19 Pollen)
1 × set of US 10 double-pointed needles
Spare US 10 double-pointed needles and sets of circular
   needles ranging in length from 12 in (30 cm) to 32
   in (80 cm) (How many you need depends on your
   knitting preference and how comfortable you are with
   crowded stitches. Many knitters use interchangeable
   needles such as Addi or Denise, which would take
   away the need for so many circulars.)
9 × stitch markers

GAUGE
16 sts and 26 rows to 4 in (10 cm) over st st
   using US 10 needles.

Note

The blanket is worked entirely in the round, from the middle outwards, increasing each edge to form a giant square.

Abbreviations

C2F: k into front of second st on needle, k into first st, slip both sts off the needle.

C2B: k into back of second st on needle, k into first st, slip both st off the needle.

Pattern

SET UP

The first step is the hardest; it's all downhill from here. Using dpns (or, if you're familiar with the magic loop method (see page 15), a very long circular needle) CO 4 sts. Divide sts evenly around dpns and join to work in the round.

First round: (k1, yf, k1) into each st, place end-of-round marker. 12 sts/3 sts per set.

Next round: p to end.

Next round: *k1, m1, pm, k1, pm, m1, k1, repeat from * to end of round. 20 sts/5 sts per set.

GARTER STITCH SECTION

Next round: p to end.

Next round: *k to marker, m1, sl marker, k1, sl marker, m1, repeat from * to end of round (28 sts/7 sts per set). Repeat last 2 rows until there are 60 sts/ 15 per set.

Change to your shortest set of circular needles when you have 60 stitches. Repeat last two rows until there are 100 sts/25 sts per set.

STOCKINETTE-STITCH SECTION

Next round: *k to end.

Next round: *k to marker, m1, sl marker, k1, sl marker, m1, repeat from * to end of round. 108 sts/27 sts per set.

Repeat last two rows until there are 188 sts/47 sts per set.

HONEYCOMB SECTION

Next round: *C2F, C2B, repeat from * to end of round.

Next round: *k to marker, m1, sl marker, k1, sl marker, m1, repeat from * to end of round. 196 sts/49 sts per set.

Next round: *C2B, C2F, repeat from * to end of round.

Next round: *k to marker, m1, sl marker, k1, sl marker, m1, repeat from * to end of round. 204 sts/51 per set.

Repeat last 4 rounds until there are 252 sts/63sts per set, ensuring you keep markers in place. Do not work the first st after the marker into the cable pattern, but work it in st st. Also, work increased sts in st st until you have 2 unincorporated stitches. Then, on the following cable round, work them either a CRB or C2F as appropriate. Work another st st section until there are 300 sts/75 sts per set.

Work another garter-stitch section until there are 324 sts/81 sts per set.

Work another st st section until there are 372 sts/93 sts per set.

Work another honeycomb section until there are 404 sts/101 sts per set.

Work another st st section until there are 420 sts / 105 sts per set.

Work another garter-stitch section until there are 508 sts / 127 sts per set.

Cast off very loosely purlwise (you may want to switch to a larger size needle if you have one handy).

Weave in ends.

Finishing

Dunk the blanket in a sink full of lukewarm water, then lay it flat to dry on a towel, pulling the corners out to form a square. Make sure that each concentric square is suitably squarish when you lay it out to dry. Don't stretch it out too far – there's no need to force it to be huge, and you don't want to distort the honeycomb pattern.

baby cozy

Since Maile was a winter baby, I felt
I had to knit her lots of warmth. My house
can be fairly cold, so I wanted to make
her something toasty, snuggly and protective.
This is essentially a sleeping bag, and it
turned out to be ideal as she was always
kicking off her blankets.

SIZES 0–3 (3–6, 6–12) months
Shown in 6–12 months.

MATERIALS
3 x 1¾ oz balls Debbie Bliss Glen
(shade: 08 Light Blue and Silver Marl) for cozy
1 x 1¾ oz ball Debbie Bliss Glen
(shade: 08 Light Blue and Silver Marl) for hat
1 x set of US 10.5 circular needles
1 x set of US 11 double-pointed needles
Tapestry needle and needle and thread
Stitch markers
11 x 18 mm buttons
1 x 20 mm button

GAUGE
For snuggle: 14.5 sts and 22 rows over 4 in (10 cm)
   over st st using US 10.5 needles
For hat: 16 sts and 19 rows over 4 in (10 cm) over st
   st using US 11 needles.

Pattern

Using the circular needles, CO 32 sts.

Work in garter stitch for 2 rows.

Next row: k2, yf, k2, *m1, k2, repeat from * to end. 47 sts.

Work in garter stitch for 2 rows.

Next row: k2, yf, k4, m1, *k3, m1, repeat from * to last 2 sts, k2. 62 sts.

Work in garter stitch for 2 rows.

Next row: k2, yf, k6, m1, *k4, m1, repeat from * to last 2 sts, k2. 77 sts.

Work in garter stitch for 2 rows.

Next row: k2, yf, k8, m1, *k5, m1, repeat from * to last 2 sts, end k2. 92 sts.

Work in garter stitch for 3rows.

Next row: cast off 4 sts at the beginning of row, k to end. 88 sts. Do not turn.

BODY

Next row: Join to begin working in the round. Work 68 sts, then pm for end of round. Work in st st until st st section measures 11⅕ in (30 cm). Work in garter stitch for 4 in (10 cm), ending with a p round.

FLAP

Next row: cast off 43 sts, k to end. 45 sts.

Work garter stitch in rows, not rounds, for 2 in (6 cm), ending with a WS row.

Buttonhole row: k4, *yf, k2tog, k4, repeat from * to last 5 sts, yf, k2tog, k3.

Work for 3 rows in garter stitch.

Cast off all sts.

Finishing
Weave in ends. Sew 18mm buttons opposite buttonholes; at neckline, they will move increasingly away from the edge.

Hat
Using dpns, CO 4 sts.

Work i-cord (see page 14) for 4 rows.

Divide sts evenly onto 4 dpns, and join to work in the round.

Next round: kf&b into every st. 8 sts.

Next round: k 1 round.

Next round: kf&b into every st. 16 sts.

Next round: k to end.

Next round: Knit 1 round.

Next round: (K to end of needle, m1 in space between needles) around. Repeat from * until you have 48 stitches.

K for 6 rounds.

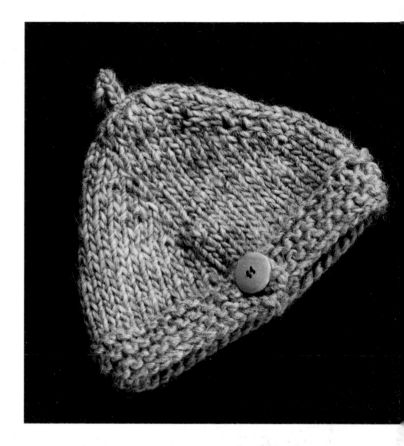

Next round: Using backward-loop cast-on method (see page 13), CO 4 sts, p to end of row. Do not join, but turn piece to work in rows.

Next row: p to end

Next row: p2, yo, p2tog, p to end.

Work in garter stitch for 3 rows.

Cast off loosely.

Finishing
Weave in ends. Sew 20 mm button opposite buttonhole.

bloomers

A frilly, old-fashioned pair of bloomers with a lace ruffle. Note: one leg is worked from the bottom up to crotch height using straight needles, then the second leg is worked in the same way, only using the circular needles to work in rows, not rounds. Then both legs are joined onto the circular needles, and worked in the round.

SIZES 0–3 (3–6, 6–12) months
(shown in 0–3 and 6–12 months).

MATERIALS
2 balls Debbie Bliss Cashmerino Aran
  (Shade: 603 Pink)
1 × pair of US 8 needles
1 × set of US 8 circular needles
Stitch holder
Tapestry needle
½ in-wide (1.5 cm) elastic
Needle and thread
1 × 18 mm button

GAUGE
21 sts and 28 rows over 4 in (10 cm) over st st
  using US 8 needles.

Pattern

EDGING (MAKE 2)

Using straight needles, CO 4 sts.

Set-up row: k to end.

Row 1: k2, yf, k2, yf, k2. 6 sts.

Row 2: k3, p1, k2

Row 3: k to end.

Row 4: sl 1, cast off 2 sts, k3. 4 sts.

Repeat rows 1–4 until piece measures 7 in/18 cm (8 in/20 cm, 8½ in/22 cm).

Cast off all sts.

LEGS

Row 1: using straight needles, pick up 34 (38, 42) sts along top of unscalloped edge.

Next row (WS): k to end.

Next row (RS): k to end.

Next row (WS): k to end.

Work 4 (4, 6) rows in st st, starting with a k row. Leg measures 2⅕ (2⅕, 2⅓) in**

Set aside.

Work second leg as first until ** using circular needles.

JOIN LEGS

Next row: k across second leg. Using the backward-loop cast-on method (see page 13), CO 4 sts, k across first leg, CO 4 sts, pm, then join to work in the round. 76 (84, 92) sts..

Work in st st for 6 in/16 cm (7 in/18 cm, 8 in/20 cm).

MAKE WAISTBAND

Next round: p to end of round.

Work ¾ in (2 cm) in st st.

Break yarn, leaving a long tail.

Finishing

Cut elastic to 16 in/40 cm (16½ in/42 cm, 17 in/44 cm). Fold into a circle with a ¾ in (2 cm) overlap. Using needle and thread, stitch down overlap.

Using your tapestry needle, and the long tail at the waistband edge, hem elastic into waistband as follows. Thread tapestry needle through live st on knitting needle, and remove st from knitting needle. Then reach around elastic with the tapestry needle, and thread tapestry needle through the corresponding st 1½ in (4 cm) below. Thread tapestry needle through another live st, remove st from knitting needle, and reach around elastic with tapestry needle to thread tapestry needle through the corresponding st. Repeat until all elastic is sewn into the waistband.

Sew crotch and leg seams together.

Sew button onto waistband as pictured.

Weave in ends.

shorts

For a manlier look, a pair of cool shorts. Note: one leg is worked from the bottom up to crotch height using straight needles, then the second leg is worked in the same way, only using the circular needles to work in rows, not rounds. Then both legs are joined onto the circular needles, and worked in the round.

SIZES 0–3 (3–6, 6–12) months (shown in 6–12 months)

MATERIALS
2 × 1¾ oz balls Debbie Bliss Cashmerino Aran (Shade: 205 Periwinkle)
1 × pair of US 8 needles
1 × set of US 8 circular needles
Stitch holder
Tapestry needle
½ in-wide (1.5 cm) elastic elastic
Needle and thread
1 × 18 mm button

GAUGE
21 sts and 28 rows over 4 in (10 cm) over st st using US 8 needles.

Pattern

LEGS

Using straight needles, CO 40 (46, 52) sts.

Next row: p to end.

Next row: k to end.

P 2 rows.

Next row: k to end.

P 2 rows.

Next row: k to end.

P 2 rows.

Work 4 (4, 6) rows in st st, starting with a k row. Leg measures 1¾ (1¾, 2) in.**
Work second leg as first until ** using circular needles.

JOIN LEGS

Next row: k across second leg. Using the backward-loop cast-on method (see page 13), CO 4 sts, k across first leg, CO 4 sts, pm, then join to work in the round. 76 (84, 92) sts.

Work in st st for 6 in/16 cm (7 in/18 cm, 8 in/20 cm).

MAKE WAISTBAND

Next round: p to end of round.

Work ¾ in (2 cm) in st st.

Break yarn, leaving a long tail.

Finishing

Cut elastic to 16 in/40 cm (16½/42 cm, 17 in/44 cm). Fold into a circle with a ¾ in (2 cm) overlap. Using needle and thread, stitch down overlap.

Using your tapestry needle, and the long tail at the waistband edge, hem elastic into waistband as follows. Thread tapestry needle through live st on knitting needle, and remove st from knitting needle. Then reach around elastic with the tapestry needle, and thread tapestry needle through the corresponding st 1½ in (4 cm) below. Thread tapestry needle through another live st, remove st from knitting needle, and reach around elastic with tapestry needle to thread tapestry needle through the corresponding st. Repeat until all elastic is sewn into the waistband.

Sew crotch and leg seams together.

Sew button onto waistband as pictured.

Weave in ends.

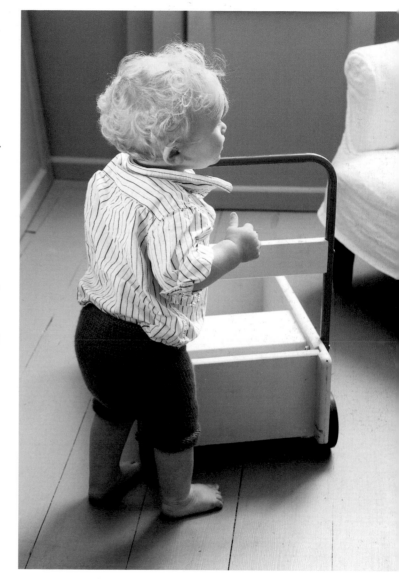

the second trimester

*Things get a little more exciting now—as your baby
bump grows so your knitting options grow with it.
If you choose to, you can explore frilly, feminine patterns
like a tutu, and a mock-pleated dress, or stick with more
versatile (and practical) cardigans and sweaters.*

Maile sweater

This is a very personal pattern, in the sense that it was designed especially for my daughter. A maile is a fragrant vine native to Hawaii, and it is traditionally used for a very special kind of lei (flower garland); my husband and I wore maile leis on our wedding day. The lei is traditionally worn open, draped over the shoulders, and the leaf pattern in this sweater echoes that.

SIZES 0–3 (3–6, 6–12) months
(shown in 3–6 months)

MATERIALS
1 × 3½ oz skein Madelinetosh Tosh Sock
    (shade: Kale). Alternatively, Dream in Color
    Smooshy, Malabrigo Yarn Sock or Plymouth
    Yarn Sock Happy Feet.
1 × set of US 4 circular needles
1 × set of US 4 double-pointed needles (optional)
3 × stitch holders, or spare yarn
Several stitch markers
4 × 15 mm buttons

GAUGE
26 sts and 36 rows to 4 in (10 cm) over st st
    using US 4 needles.

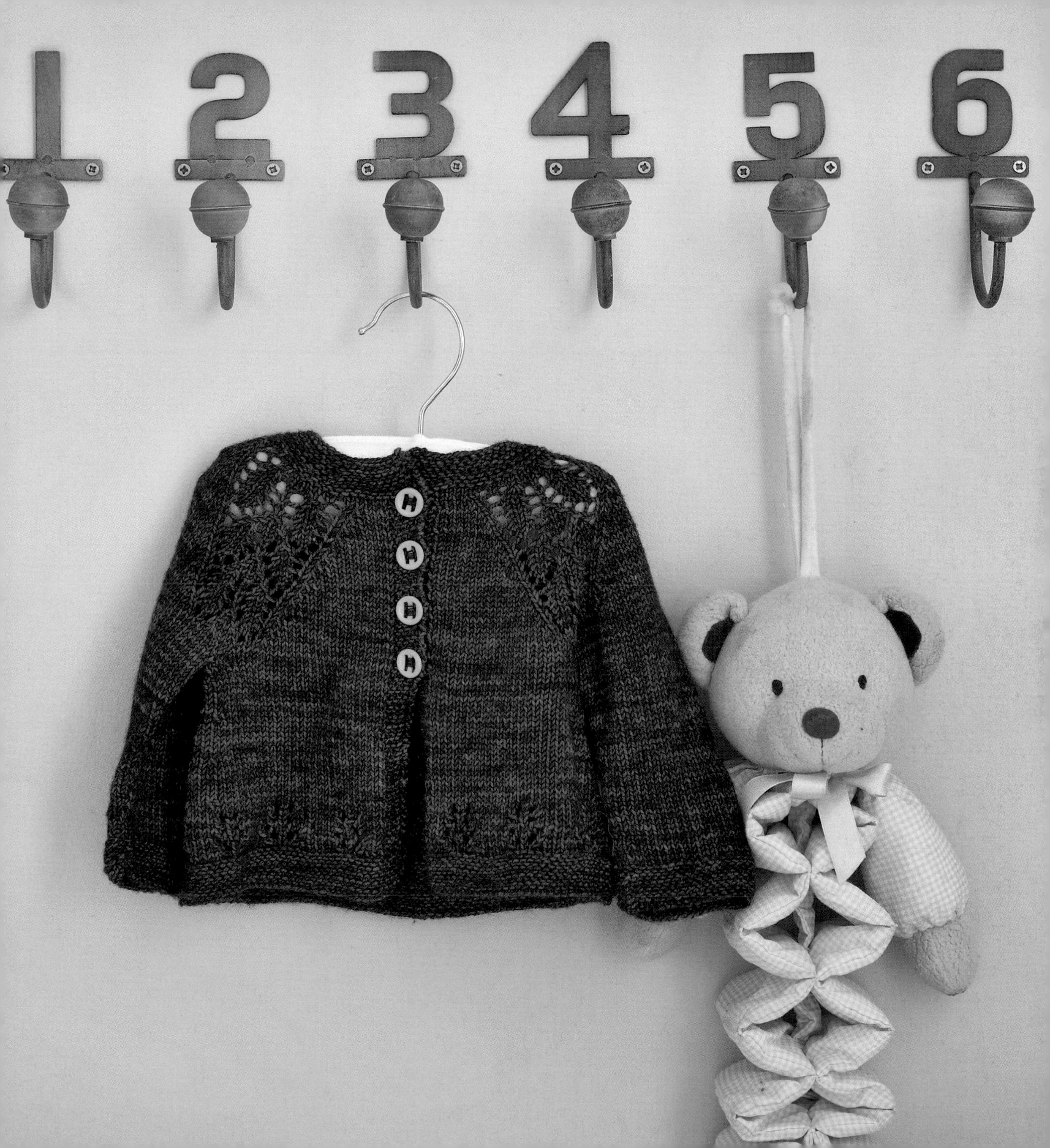
1
2
3
4
5
6

Lace pattern 1

Rows 1, 5 and 7: k3, k2tog, yf, k1, yf, sl 1 k1 psso, *k5, k2tog, yf, k1, yf, sl 1 k1 psso, repeat from * to last 3 sts, k3.

Rows 2, 4 and 6: p to end.

Row 3: k2, k2tog, yf, k3, yf, sl 1 k1 psso, *k3, k2tog, yf, k3, yf, sl 1 k1 psso, repeat from * to last 2 sts, k2.

Lace pattern 2

Row 1: (k1, yf) x 2, sl 1 k2tog psso, k3, k3tog, (yf, k1) x 2. 13 stitches.

Row 2, 4, 6, 8 and 10: p to end.

Row 3: k1, yf, k3, yf, sl 1 k1 psso, k1, k2tog, yf, k3, yf, k1. 15 stitches.

Row 5: k1, yf, sl 1 k1 psso, k1, k2tog, yf, sl 1 k2tog psso, yf, sl 1 k1 psso, k1, k2tog, yf, k1. 13 stitches.

Row 7 and 9: k1 (yf, sl 1 k1 psso, k1, k2tog, yf, k1) x 2.

Pattern

BODY

Using US 4 circular needle, CO 131 (141, 151) sts.

Working back and forth, work in garter stitch for 11 rows.

Next row WS: k5, p to last 5 sts, k5.

Next row RS: k5, work lace pattern no.1 to last 5 sts, k5.

Repeat from * working k5 at each end of rows 2, 4 and 6 as set, until all 7 rows of lace pattern no.1 have been completed.

Next row (WS): k5, p to last 5 sts, k5.

Next row: k33 (35, 37), pm, k65 (71, 77), pm, k33 (35, 37).

Next row: k5, p to last 5 sts, k5.

***Next row:** (k to 3 sts before marker, sl sl k, k1, sl marker, k1, k2tog) x 2, k to end. 127 (137, 147) sts. Work 7 (9, 11) rows straight, keeping borders as set.

Repeat from ** 2 times more. 119 (129, 139) sts.

Work straight as set until piece measures 4½ in/11 cm (5 in/13 cm, 6 in/15 cm), ending with a RS row.

Next row (WS): (k5, p to 2 sts before marker, cast off 4 sts) x 2, p to last 5 sts, k5. 111 (121, 131) sts.

Place these sts on a holder.

SLEEVE (MAKE 2)

Using US 4 circular needle, CO 34 (38, 42) sts.

Working back and forth, work in garter stitch for 10 rows.

***Next row (RS):** k2, m1, k to last 2 sts, m1, k2. 36 (40, 44) sts.

Work 3 (5, 5) rows in st st.

Repeat from * 3 times more. 42, (46, 50) sts.

****Next row (RS):** k2, m1, k to last 2 sts, m1, k2. 44 (48, 52) sts.

Work 5 (5, 7) rows in st st.

Repeat from ** 2 times more. 48 (52, 56) sts.

Work straight as set until piece measures 5 in/12 cm (6 in/15 cm, 7 in/18 cm), ending with a WS row.

Cast off 2 sts at the beginning of the next two rows 44, (48, 52) sts.

Place these sts on a holder.

YOKE

Place body sts back on needle. With RS facing k to 6 sts before 4 cast-off sts, pm, k6, k7 sts of first sleeve, pm, k to end of sleeve, pm, k body sts until you reach the cast-off sts, pm, k to 7 sts before the end of the second sleeve, pm, k7, k6 sts of body, pm, k to the end of body. 199 (217, 235) sts. (Note: This is a tight, and tricky sleeve join. If you are familiar with the magic loop knitting method (see page 15), pulling the excess wire with your right hand, and bending the wire to bring the sts closer together will save your hands, and needles some trouble. Alternatively, you can slide the sleeve sts onto your optional dpns, which will give you a little more space to work with.)

Buttonhole row: k5, p to last 5 sts, k1, k2tog, yf, k2.

*Next row (RS): *k to 2 sts before marker, sl sl k, work lace pattern 2 between markers, k2tog, (k to 3 sts before marker, sl sl k, k2, k2tog) × 2, k to 2 sts before marker, sl sl k, work lace pattern 2 between markers, k2tog, k to end.

Next row: k5, p to last 5 sts, k5.

Repeat from * until you have worked lace pattern 2, 3 times in total, working a buttonhole every 10 rows. 87 (105, 123) sts.

0–3 MONTHS ONLY
Next row: k to end.

Next row: k to last 4 sts, k2tog, yf, k2.

Next row: *k12 , k2tog repeat from * to last 3 sts, k3. 81 sts.

Next row: k to end.

Next row: *k11, k2tog repeat from * to last 3 sts, k3. 75 sts.

Next row: k to end.

Next row: *k10, k2tog. Repeat from * to last 3 sts, k3. 69 sts.

Next row: k to end.

Next row: *k9, k2tog. Repeat from * to last 3 sts, k3. 63 sts.

3–6 MONTHS ONLY

Work 2 more rows as established, including a buttonhole row. 97 sts.

Next row: *k14, k2tog, repeat from * to last st, k1. 91 sts.

Next row: k to end.

Next row: *k13, k2tog, repeat from * to last st, k1. 85 sts.

Next row: k to end.

Next row: *k12, k2tog, repeat from * to last st, k1. 79 sts.

Next row: k to end.

Next row: *k11, k2tog, repeat from * to last st, k1. 73 sts.

Next row: k to end.

Next row: *k10, k2tog, repeat from * to last st, k1. 67 sts.

Next row: k to end.

6–12 MONTHS ONLY

Work 4 more rows as established, including a buttonhole row. 107 sts.

Next row: *k15, k2tog. Repeat from * to last 5 sts, k5. 101 sts.

Next row: k to end.

Next row: *k14, k2tog. Repeat from * to last 5 sts, k5. 95 sts.

Next row: k to end.

Next row: *k13, k2tog. Repeat from * to last 5 sts, k5. 89 sts.

Next row: k to end.

Next row: *k12, k2tog. Repeat from * to last 5 sts, k5 83 sts.

Next row: k to end.

Next row: *k11, k2tog. Repeat from * to last 5 sts, k5 77 sts.

Next row: k to end.

ALL SIZES

Cast off all sts.

Finishing

Weave in ends. Sew sleeve seams and stitch underarms.

Block lightly. Sew buttons opposite buttonholes.

striped boatneck sweater

Both the back and front of this sweater are worked in exactly the same way. In fact, the construction is as simple as it could possibly be, but the lovely texture of the yarn and the bold stripe pattern make it stand out, while its wide neck, light weight, and roomy fit make it comfortable and practical.

SIZES 0–3 (3–6, 6–12) months
(shown in 6–12 months)

MATERIALS
1 (2, 3) × 1¾ oz balls Rowan Felted Tweed DK
   (shade: 165 Scree) for MC
1 (1, 2) × 1¾ oz balls Rowan Felted Tweed DK
   (shade: 159 Carbon) for CC
1 × pair US 6 needles
Tapestry needle

GAUGE
19.5 sts and 31.5 rows to 4 in (10 cm) over double
   seed st. using US 6 needles.

Pattern

BACK/FRONT (MAKE 2)

Using MC, CO 49 (53, 57) sts.

Work in double seed stitch for 4 (8, 8) rows as follows:

Rows 1 and 4 (RS): k1, *p1, k1, repeat from * to end.

Rows 2 and 3: p1, *k1, p1, repeat from * to end.

0–3 AND 6–12 MONTHS ONLY

Work rows 1 and 2 of double seed stitch pattern.

ALL SIZES

*Change to CC. Work 6 (8, 10) rows in st st.

Change to MC. Work 6 (8, 10) rows in st st.

Repeat from * until 5th (4th, 4th) CC stripe is complete.

Using MC, work straight in double seed stitch until piece measures 8½ in/21 cm (10 in, 11 in/25 cm, 28 cm), ending with a WS row.

Next row (RS): work 12 (14, 15) sts in pattern, cast off 25 (25, 27) sts, work to end (of left shoulder).

Leaving sts for left shoulder on the needle, and continuing with double seed stitch pattern as set, work right shoulder for 1 in/2.5 cm (1 in/2.75 cm, 1⅕ in/3 cm).

Next row: Cast off right shoulder sts.

Next row: Attach yarn and work left shoulder in double seed stitch pattern as set to match right shoulder.

Cast off left shoulder sts.

SLEEVE (MAKE 2)

Using MC, CO 30 (34, 36) sts.

Work in double seed stitch for 6 (8, 10) rows as follows:

Rows 1 and 2 (RS): *k1, p1, repeat from * to end.

Rows 3 and 4: *p1, k1, repeat from * to end.

Change to CC. Continue to work in st st, in stripe pattern as set for back/front, with 6 (8, 10) rows per color.

At the same time, work increases as follows:

*Work 7 (7, 8) rows even in st st.

Next row: work 2, m1, work to 2 sts before end, m1, work 2.

Repeat from * 6 times more. 44 (48, 50) sts.

Work 2 (4, 2) rows straight.

Cast off all sts.

Finishing

Weave in ends.

Using MC, sew shoulder and sleeve seams. Starting at bottom hem, sew to 4 in/10 cm (4½ in/12 cm, 5 in/13 cm) from shoulder seam. Set sleeves into armholes.

Block lightly as desired.

Sophie blouse

My niece Sophie is two days younger than my daughter Maile, but Maile has been chasing after her from the very beginning. Sophie walked first, she talked first, and she always had the coolest clothes. This ruched top would look great with Sophie's signature jeans and her classic Mary Jane shoes.

SIZES 0–3 (3–6, 6–12) months (shown in 6–12 months).

MATERIALS
1 x 1¾ oz skein Punta Mericash Solid
   (shade: Pale Lavendar)
1 x set of US 6 16 in circular needles
Stitch markers
1 x set of US 6 double-pointed needles, a cable
   needle or spare US 6 needle
3 x 15 mm buttons
Needle and thread

GAUGE
25 sts and 36 rows to 4 in (10 cm) over st st
   using US 6 needles.

Pattern

BLOUSE

CO 63 (56, 62) sts. Work back and forth on circular needle.

Row 1 (RS): p12 (11, 12), pm, p9 (7, 8), pm, p21 (20, 22), pm, p9 (7, 8) pm, p12 (11, 12).

Row 2 (WS): k to end.

RAGLAN SECTION

Row 1 (RS): p4, (k to marker, m1, sl marker, k1, m1) × 4, k to last 4 sts, p. 72 (64, 70) sts.

Row 2: p2, yb, p2tog, p to second marker, sl marker, pf&b into every st until last st before third marker, p1, sl marker, p to end. 95 (85, 93) sts.

Row 3: as row 1. 103 (93, 101) sts.

Row 4: p to end.

Row 5: as row 1. 111 (101, 109) sts.

Row 6: p to end.

Row 7: as row 1. 119 (109, 117) sts.

3–6 AND 6–12 MONTHS ONLY
Row 8: p to end.

Row 9: as row 1. (117, 125sts.)

ALL SIZES
Row 10: p to second marker, sl marker, p2tog to 1 st before third marker, p1, p to end. 92 (91, 97) sts.

Row 11: p4, k to marker, m1, sl marker, k1, m1, k to next marker, m1, sl marker, k1, m1p, p to next marker, m1p, sl marker, k1, m1, k to next marker, m1, sl marker, k1, m1, k to last 4 sts, p to end. 100 (99, 105) sts.

Row 12: p to second marker, sl marker, k to 1 st before third marker, p1, p to end.

Repeat last 10 (12, 12) rows 2 times more. 174 (188, 194) sts.

SLEEVE FOR 0–3 MONTHS ONLY

Row 13: p4, k to first marker, m1, sl marker, (p4, p2tog) × 6, p3, sl marker, k1, m1, k to third marker, m1, sl marker, p3, (p2tog, p4) × 6, sl marker, k1, m1, k to last 4 sts, p4.

Row 14: p to end.

Row 15: p4, k to first marker, m1, sl marker, (p3, p2tog) × 6, p3, sl marker, k1, m1, k to third marker, m1, sl marker, p3 (p2tog, p3) × 6, sl marker, k1, m1, k to last 4 sts, p4.

Row 16: removing markers as you go, p to 1st marker, cast off knitwise to second marker, p to third marker, cast off knitwise to 4th marker, p to end. 106 sts.

SLEEVE FOR 3—6 MONTHS ONLY

Row 13: p4, k to first marker, m1, sl marker, (p6, p2tog) × 5, p3, sl marker, k1, m1, k to third marker, m1, sl marker, p3 (p2tog, p6) × 5, sl marker, k1, m1, k to last 4 sts, p4.

Row 14: p to end.

Row 15: p4, k to first marker, m1, sl marker, (p5, p2tog) × 5, p3, sl marker, k1, m1, k to third marker, m1, sl marker, p3 (p2tog, p5) × 5, sl marker, k1, m1, k to last 4 sts, p4.

Row 16: removing markers as you go, p to first marker, cast off knitwise to second marker, p to third marker, cast off knitwise to fourth marker, p to end. 110 sts.

SLEEVE FOR 6—12 MONTHS ONLY

Row 13: p4, k to first marker, m1, sl marker, p6, p2tog (p4, p2tog) × 5, p6, sl marker, k1, m1, k to third marker, m1, sl marker, p6, p2tog (p4, p2tog) × 5, p6, sl marker, k1, m1, k to last 4 sts, p4.

Row 14: p to end.

Row 15: p4, k to first marker, m1, sl marker, p5, p2tog, (p3, p2tog) × 5, p6, sl marker, k1, m1, k to third marker, m1, sl marker, p6, p2tog, (p3, p2tog) × 5, p5, sl marker, k1, m1, k to last 4 sts, p4.

Row 16: removing markers as you go, p to first marker, cast off knitwise to second marker, p to third marker, cast off knitwise to fourth marker, p to end. 114 sts.

ALL SIZES

Next row: p4, (k to gap where sleeve sts have been cast off and, using backward-loop cast-on method (see page 13) CO 3 (4, 4) sts, pm, CO 3 (4, 4) sts) × 2, k to last 4 sts and STOP. Slip next 4 sts onto dpn. Slide sts on

circular needle to other end of circular needle, so as to join in the round. Holding dpn in front, *p2tog first st from needle and first st from dpn *. Repeat from * to * once, place end-of-round marker, repeat from * to * twice more. 114 (122, 126) sts.

*K 6 rounds.

Next round: (k to 1st before side marker, m1, k1, sl marker, k1, m1) × 2, k to end.

Repeat from * 4 (5,6) times more. 134 (146, 154) sts. Work even until piece measures 9 in/23 cm (10.5 in/26.5 cm, 11.5 in/28.5 cm).

P 3 rounds.
Cast off all sts purlwise.

Finishing

Sew buttons opposite buttonholes. Weave in ends.

tutu

The first time I showed my daughter a tutu, she immediately wanted to wear it. Now, please! Some girls are like that, while others would never be caught dead in something so pink and fluffy. You just never know…

SIZES 0–3 (3–6, 6–12) months
(shown in 3–6 months)

MATERIALS
2 × ⅞ oz balls Debbie Bliss Angel
  (shade: 15 Pale Pink)
1 × 1¾ oz ball Debbie Bliss Cashmerino Aran
  (shade: 043 Baby Pink)
1 × pair of US 10 needles
1 × set of US 10 circular needles
Tapestry needle
½ in-wide (1.5 cm) piece of elastic
Needle and thread

GAUGE
16 sts and 22 rows to 4 in (10 cm) over garter stitch
  using Angel yarn and US 10 needles.

Pattern

Using straight needles and Angel yarn double, CO 148 (156, 164) sts.

Next row (WS): k to end.

Next row: k1, *yf, k2tog, repeat from * to last st, k1.

Work in garter stitch for 5½ in/14 cm (6 in, 6½ in/15 cm, 16 cm), ending with a RS row.

Next row (WS): *k2tog, repeat from * to end. 74 (78, 82) sts. Break yarn and set aside.

Using circular needles and Angel yarn double, CO 148 (156, 164) sts.

Next row (WS): working back and forth k to end.

Next row: k1, *yf, k2tog, repeat from * to last st, k1.

Work in garter stitch for 4 in/10 cm (4½ in/11 cm, 5 in/12 cm), ending with a RS row.

Next row (WS): *k2tog, repeat from * to end. 74 (78, 82) sts.

Holding circular needle, and straight needle parallel in your left hand, with the circular needle in front, *k 1 st from circular needle together with 1 st from straight needle onto circular needle * to join the two layers of the tutu. Repeat from * to * to end. Join to work in the round.

Next round: Attach Cashmerino yarn and knit the Angel and Cashmerino together in st st for 1 in/3 cm (this creates a nice thick waistband).

Next round: p to end.

Work in st st for 1 in (3 cm). Break yarn, leaving a long tail of Cashmerino. Set aside.

Finishing

Cut elastic to 16 in/40 cm (16½ in/42 cm, 17 in/44 cm). Fold into a circle with a ¾ in (2 cm) overlap. Using the needle and thread, stitch down overlap.

Using your tapestry needle and the long Cashmerino tail at the waistband edge, hem elastic into waistband. Thread the tapestry needle through a live st on the knitting needle and remove st from knitting needle. Then reach around elastic with the tapestry needle and thread the tapestry needle through the corresponding st at beginning of the st st section. Thread tapestry needle through another live st, remove st from knitting needle, and reach around elastic with the tapestry needle to thread tapestry needle through the corresponding st at beginning of st st section. Repeat until entire elastic circle is sewn into the waistband.

Sew sides of both tutu layers together. Weave in ends.

cuffed pants

Comfy yet attractive baby pants are hard to come by—you're either stuck with tapered leggings or you have to struggle to ease your squirming baby into a pair of chinos with every diaper change. These pants have a loose elastic waistband, a roomy fit and are extremely soft.

SIZES 0–3 (3–6, 6–12) months (shown in 3–6 months).

MATERIALS
2 (2, 3) × 1¾ oz balls Rowan Cashsoft DK (shade: 505 Mist)
1 × set of US 6 12 in circular needles
1 × stitch holder
1 × stitch marker
Tapestry needle and needle and thread
½ in-wide piece of elastic
1 × 19 mm button
2 × 11.5 mm buttons

GAUGE
22 sts and 30 rows to 4 in (10 cm) over seed st using US 6 needles.

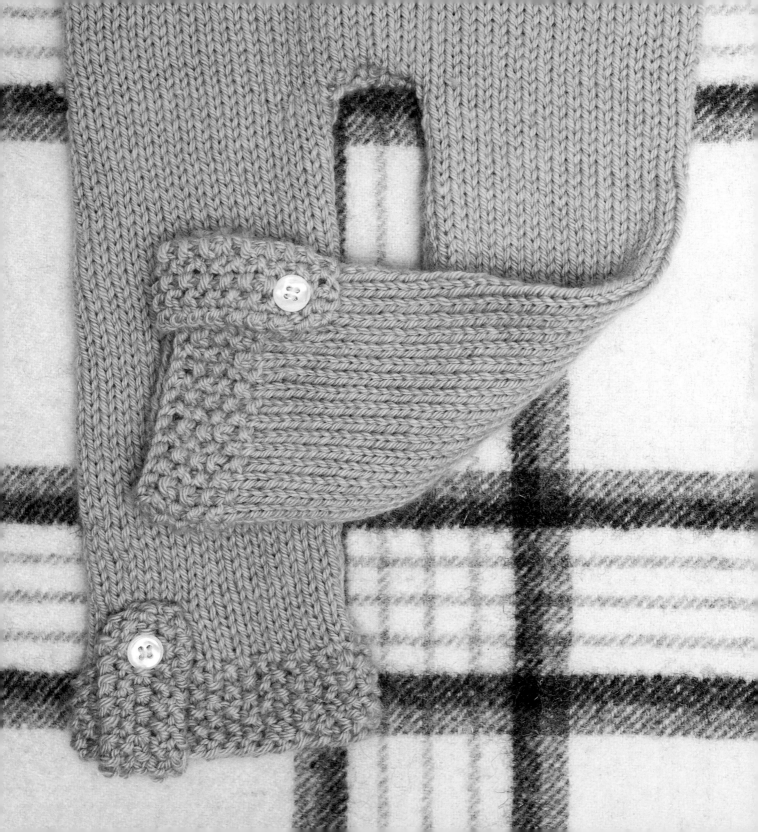

Pattern

LEGS (MAKE 2)

CO 42 (46, 50) sts, leaving a long tail.

Next row (RS): working back and forth work in seed stitch as follows:

Row 1: *k1, p1, repeat from * to end.

Row 2: * p1, k1, repeat from * to end.

Repeat these 2 rows 3 times more.

Work straight in st st until piece measures 7 in/18 cm (8 in, 9 in/20 cm, 22 cm), ending with a WS row.

First leg only: place sts on a holder.

Second leg only: leave sts on the needle.

JOIN LEGS

K second-leg sts on the needle, CO 4 sts using backward loop method (see page 13), k across first-leg sts on holder, CO 4 sts. 92 (100, 108) sts. Place marker and join to work in the round.

Work straight in the round for 5½ in/14 cm (6 in/16 cm, 7 in/18 cm).

Next round: *k2, p2, repeat from * to end.

Continue in double rib for 2 in (6 cm).

Break yarn, leaving a long tail. Set aside.

TABS (MAKE 2)

CO 5 sts. (Note: see magic loop knitting, page 15), for knitting small amounts of sts on circular needles.)

Next row: work in seed stitch as follows: *k1, p1, repeat from * to last st, k1.

Repeat this row for 4 in.

Cast off all sts.

Finishing

Cut elastic to 16 in/40 cm (16½ in /42 cm, 17 in / 44 cm). Fold into a circle, with a ¾ in (2 cm) overlap. Using needle and thread, stitch down overlap.

Using your tapestry needle, and the long tail at the waistband edge, hem elastic into waistband. Thread the tapestry needle through a live st on the knitting needle and remove st from knitting needle. Then reach around elastic with the tapestry needle, and thread the tapestry needle through the corresponding st at the beginning of the ribbing. Thread the tapestry needle through another live st, remove the st from the knitting needle, and reach around the elastic with the tapestry needle to thread the tapestry needle through the corresponding rib st. Repeat until entire elastic circle is sewn into the waistband.

Sew crotch and leg seams.

Sew tabs at cuffs as pictured.

Sew 19 mm button onto waistband and 11.5 mm buttons onto tabs.

Weave in ends.

Block lightly as desired.

little old man cardigan

Very young babies often look more like old men than cherubs. My grandfather often wore a cardigan like this one, which I designed with my cousin Chris's particularly elderly-looking son, Marek, in mind.

SIZES 0–3 (3–6, 6–12) months (shown in 3–6 months)

MATERIALS
2 (2, 3) × 1¾ oz balls Rowan Cashsoft DK
   (shade: 517 Donkey)
1 × pair of US 7 needles
4 × stitch markers
2 × stitch holders or spare yarn
Tapestry needle
2 × 20 mm buttons
Needle and thread

GAUGE
22 sts and 30 rows to 4 in (10 cm) over st st using
   US 7 needles.

Pattern

NECKLINE

CO 28 sts.

Row 1 (WS): k3, pm, k4, pm, k14, pm, k4, pm, k3.

Row 2 (raglan row 1): (k to 1 st before marker, m1, k1, sl marker, k1, m1) X 4, k to end. 36 sts.

Row 3: k to end.

Row 4: raglan row 1. 44 sts.

Row 5: k to end.

Row 6: raglan row 1. 52 sts.

YOKE:

*Row 1 (WS): k5, p to last 5 sts, k5.

Row 2 (raglan row 2): k to 1 st after first marker, m1, (k to 1 st before marker, m1, k1, sl marker, k1, m1) x 2, k to 1 st before last marker, m1, k to end. 58 sts.

Row 3: k5, p to last 5 sts, k5.

Row 4: (k to 1 st before marker, m1, k1, sl marker, k1, m1) x 4, k to end. 66 sts.

Repeat from * until there are 156 sts, ending with a raglan row 2.

BODY

0–3 MONTHS

Next row (WS): k5, p to first marker, place next 40 sleeve sts on holder, CO 4 sts using the backward-loop cast-on method (see page 13), p to next marker, place next 40 sleeve sts on holder, CO 4 sts using the backward-loop cast-on method, p to last 5 sts, k5. 84 sts.

3–6 MONTHS

Work rows 3, 4, 1 and 2 once more. 170 sts.

Next row: k5, p to first marker, place next 44 sts on holder for sleeve, CO 4 sts using the backward-loop cast-on method, p to next marker, place next 44 sts on holder, CO 4 sts using the backward-loop cast-on method, p to last 5 sts, k5. 90 sts.

6–12 MONTHS

Work rows 3, 4, 1 and 2 twice more. 184 sts.

Next row: k5, p to first marker, place next 48 sts on holder for sleeve, CO 4 sts using the backward-loop cast-on method, p to next marker, place next 48 sts on holder, CO 4 sts using backward-loop cast-on method, p to last 5 sts, k5. 96 sts.

ALL SIZES

**Row 1 (RS): k to end.

Row 2: k5, m1p, p to last 5 sts, m1p, k5. 82 (88, 94) sts.

Row 3: k to end.

Row 4: k5, p to last 5 sts, k5.

Repeat from ** until there are 100 (106, 112) sts, ending with a row 2. Piece measures 10 in/25.5 cm (10.5 in/27 cm, 11 in/28 cm).

Work 3 rows straight, keeping garter stitch edge as established.

Buttonhole row: work to last 4 sts, k2tog, yf, k2.

Work 6 (7, 8) rows straight.

Next row: work buttonhole row once more.

Work 3 rows straight, keeping garter edge as established. Piece measures 11.5 in/29.5 cm (12 in/31 cm, 13 in/32.5 cm). Work in garter stitch for 9rows.

Cast off all sts.

SLEEVES

Place right sleeve sts on needle.

Next row (RS): cast off 2 sts, k to end. 38 (42, 46) sts.

Next row: cast off 2 sts, p to end. 36 (40, 44) sts.

***Work 9 (10, 11) rows straight.

Next row: decrease 1 st at each end.

Repeat from *** until 28 (32, 36) sts remain.

Work even until piece measures 5.5 in/14 cm (6 in/15 cm, 6.5 in/17 cm).

ALL SIZES

Work in garter stitch for 9 rows.

Cast off all sts.

Repeat with left sleeve.

Finishing

Weave in ends. Sew sleeve seams and attach buttons opposite buttonholes.

Block lightly as desired.

Ike sweater vest

Our young friend Ike is six months older than Maile. He's an affectionate fellow and will press his forehead to yours if he likes you— Maile was instantly smitten. And best of all, he taught Maile to crawl. We had been demonstrating crawling for some time but, sometimes, you just need a professional. I designed this sweater vest with Ike in mind—something comfortable but just a little bit gentlemanly.

SIZES 0–3 (3–6, 6–12) months
(shown in 6–12 months)

MATERIALS
2 x 1¾ oz balls Rowan Cotton Glace
   (shade: 726 Bleached) for MC
1 (2, 2) balls Rowan Cotton Glace
   (shade: 834 Whey) for CC
1 x set of US 5 circular needles
1 x set of US 5 double-pointed needles
1 x stitch holder
1 x stitch marker
Tapestry needle

GAUGE
23 sts x 34 rows to 4 in (10 cm) over st st
   using US 5 needles.

Pattern

BODY

Using MC, CO 102 (108, 114) sts. Join to work in the round, and place marker to mark end of round.

Next round: *k1, p1, repeat from * to end.

Continue working in rib until piece measures 1 in (3 cm).

Drop MC, but do not break yarn. Join CC and k 2 rounds.

*Drop CC and pick up MC, k 2 rounds.

Drop MC, pick up CC, k 2 rounds.

Repeat from * until piece measures 5 in/12 cm (6 in /15 cm, 7 in/18 cm), ending with a second round of either CC or MC, ensuring that the stripe has been completed.

Work as folllows maintaining the established stripe pattern.

Next round: k45 (48, 51), cast off 6 sts, k45 (48, 51), cast off 6 sts. Place last k45 (48, 51) sts on a holder for the front.

BACK

Work back and forth in rows and maintain stripe pattern.

**Next row:* k1, sl sl k, k to 3 sts, k2tog, k1.

Next row: p to end.

Repeat from **4 times more. 35 (38, 41) sts.

Work straight until piece measures 10½ in/26 cm, (12 in/30 cm, 13½ in/34 cm), ending with a WS row.

LEFT SHOULDER

Next row (RS): k10, cast off 25 (28, 31) sts, k to end.

Next row: cast off 5 sts, p to end.

Next row (RS): k5.

Next row (WS): cast off all sts.

RIGHT SHOULDER

Attach yarn and work as for left shoulder, reversing all shaping.

Transfer sts on holder to needle. Attach yarn and begin working in rows, maintaining the stripe pattern as established.

RIGHT NECK (FRONT)

Next row (RS): k1, sl sl k, k17 (18, 19), then turn, leaving remaining sts on a holder.

***Next row:* p1, p2tog, p to end.

Next row: k1, sl sl k, k to end.

Next row: p 1 row.

Next row: k1, sl sl k, k to end.

Next row: p1, p2tog, p to end.

3–6 AND 6–12 MONTHS ONLY
Next row (RS): k1, sl sl k, to end.

Next row: p to end. 15 (15, 16) sts.

ALL SIZES
Maintain stripe pattern as established.

****Work 3 (4, 5) rows straight.

Next row (WS): decrease 1 st at neckline 14 (14, 15) sts.

Repeat from **** until 10 sts remain.

Work straight until piece measures 10½ in/26 cm (12 in/30 cm, 13½ in/34 cm), ending with a WS row.

Next row (RS): cast off 5 sts, k to end

Next row: p5.

Cast off all sts.

LEFT NECK

Maintain stripe pattern as established.

Next row (RS): attach yarn at neckline, cast off 5 (6, 7) sts, k to last 3 sts, k2tog, k1.

Work as for right neck, reversing all shaping from ***.

Finishing

Sew shoulder seams, and weave in ends.

NECKLINE

With RS facing and using MC, starting on left side of V-neck at the edge of the cast off sts, pick up and k 46 (50, 54) sts along left neckline, 24 (28, 30) sts along back neck and 46 (50, 54) sts along right neckline. 116 (128, 138) sts. Work around neckline, but DO NOT pick up the 5 (6, 7) cast off sts at the base of neck.

Row 1: *p1, k1, repeat from * to end.

Work last rows 3 (5, 5) times more. Cast off all sts in pattern.

Sew edges of rib together at base of neck and stitch flap down to cast off sts.

ARMHOLES

Using dpns and MC, pick up and k 52 (56, 60) sts around armhole. Join to work in the round, and place marker to mark end of round.

Next round: *k1, p1, repeat from * to end.

Work this round 1 (1, 2) time(s) more.

Cast off all sts in pattern.

Repeat with second armhole.

Weave in ends.

Block lightly.

autumn leaves sweater

This delicious yarn with all the colors of autumn is feminine, without being overly girly. In this pattern, I increase the size of the garment by increasing the yarn weight. So to make the smallest size I use Madelinetosh Tosh DK and US 5 needles. For medium, I use Madelinetosh Tosh DK and US 7 needles. And for the largest size, I use Madelinetosh Tosh Merino and US 9 needles. The pattern doesn't change with the size, only your needles and your yarn do!

SIZES 0–3 (3–6, 6–12) months (shown in 3–6 months)

MATERIALS
1 x 3½ oz skein Madelinetosh Tosh DK (shade: Amber Trinket), or 1 x 3½ oz skein Madelinetosh Tosh Merino
1 x set of US 5 12 in circular needles or 1 x set of US 7 circular needles or 1 x set of US 9 circular needles
Tapestry needle
4 x stitch markers
3 x 15 mm (18 mm, 20 mm) buttons
Needle and thread

GAUGE
22 sts and 30 rows to 4 in (10 cm) over st st using US 5 needles.
20 sts and 27 rows to 4 in (10 cm) over st st using US 7 needles.
18 sts and 25 rows to 4 in (10 cm) over st st using US 9 needles.

Seed stitch

Row 1: *k1, p1, repeat from * to last stitch, k1.

Row 2: Repeat this row.

Pattern

NECKLINE

CO 55 sts.

Work 2 rows in seed stitch.

Next row: k1, p1, yo, p2tog, continue in seed stitch to end of row.

Work 3 rows in seed stitch.

Autumn leaves pattern

Row 1 (WS): k1, p1, k1, p4, *k1, p3, repeat from * to last 4 sts, p1, k1, p1, k1.

Row 2: k1, p1, k1, p1, *k1, (yo, k1) x 2, p1, repeat from * to last 3 sts, k1, p1, k1. 79 sts.

Row 3: k1, p1, k1, p6, *k1, p5, repeat from * to last 4 sts, p1, k1, p1, k1.

Row 4: k1, p1, k1, p1, *k2, yo, k1, yo, k2, p1, repeat from * to last 3 sts, k1, p1, k1. 103 sts.

Row 5: k1, p1, k1, p8, *k1, p7, repeat from * to last 4 sts, p1, k1, p1, k1.

Row 6: k1, p1, k1, p1, *k7, p1, repeat from * to last 3 sts, k1, p1, k1.

Row 7: as row 5.

Row 8: k1, p1, k1, p1, *k3, yo, k1, yo, k3, p1, repeat from * to last 3 sts, end k1, p1, k1. 127 sts.

Row 9: k1, p1, k1, p10, *k1, p9, repeat from * to last 4 sts, p1, k1, p1, k1.

Row 10 (buttonhole row): k1, p1, k1, p1, *k9, p1, repeat from * to last 13 sts, k9, p2tog, yo, p1, k1.

Row 11: as row 9.

Row 12: k1, p1, k1, p1, *k4, yo, k1, yo, k4, p1, repeat from * to last 3 sts, k1, p1, k1. 151 sts.

Row 13: k1, p1, k1, p12, *k1, p11, repeat from * to last 4 sts, p1, k1, p1, k1.

Row 14: k1, p1, k1, p1, *k11, p1, repeat from * to last 3 sts, k1, p1, k1.

Row 15: as row 13.

Row 16: k1, p1, k1, *p1, yo, sl 1 k1 psso, k7, k2tog, yo, repeat from * to last 4 sts, p1, k1, p1, k1.

Row 17: k1, p1, k1, p1, k1, *p9, k3, repeat from * to last 14 sts, p9, k1, p1, k1, p1, k1.

Row 18: k1, p1, k1, p2, yf, sl 1 k1 psso, k5, k2tog, *yo, p3, yo, sl 1 k1 psso, k5, k2tog, repeat from * to last 5 sts, yo, p2, k1, p1, k1.

Row 19: k1, p1, k1, p1, k2, p7, *k2, p1, k2, p7, repeat from * to last 6 sts, k2, p1, k1, p1, k1.

Row 20: k1, p1, k1, p3, yf, sl 1 k1 psso, k3, k2tog, *yo, p2, k1, p2, yf, sl 1 k1 psso, k3, k2tog, repeat from * to last 6 sts, yo, p3, k1, p1, k1.

Row 21: k1, p1, k1, p2, k2, p5, *k2, p3, k2, p5, repeat from * to last 7 sts, k2, p2, k1, p1, k1.

Row 22: k1, p1, k1, p1, k1, p2, yb, sl 1 k1 psso, k1, k2tog, *yb, p2, k3, p2, yb, sl 1 k1 pssp, k1, k2tog, repeat from * to last 7 sts, yb, p2, k1, p1, k1, p1, k1.

Row 23 (buttonhole row): k1, p1, yo, p2tog, p2, k2, p3, *k2, p5, k2, p3, repeat from * to last 8 sts, k2, p3, k1, p1, k1.

Row 24: k1, p1, k1, p1, k2, p2, yo, sl 1 k2tog psso, *yo, p2, k5, p2, yo, sl 1 k2tog psso, repeat from * to last 8 sts, yo, p2, k2, p1, k1, p1, k1.

Row 25: k1, p1, k1, p4, k2, p1, *k2, p7, k2, p1, repeat from * to last 9 sts, k2, p4, k1, p1, k1.

Row 26: k1, p1, k1, p1, k to last 4 sts, p1, k1, p1, k1. 151 sts. Piece measures 4 in/10.5 cm (4.75 in, 5 in/12 cm, 13 cm).

BACK AND SIDES

Next row: k1, p1, k1, p15, sl next 36 sts onto a stitch holder. Using the backward-loop cast-on method (see page 13) CO 8 sts p43, slip next 36 sts onto stitch holder, CO 8 sts, p15, k1, p1, k1. 95 sts.

Next row: k1, p1, k1, p1, k17, pm, k49, pm, k17, p1, k1, p1, k1.

*Work 4 rows straight, keeping 4 edge sts in seed stitch as established.

Next row: k1, p1, k1, p1 (k to marker, m1, sl marker, k1, m1) x 2, k to last 4 sts, p1, k1, p1, k1. 97 sts. Repeat from * 5 times more. 117 sts.

Work 6 rows in seed stitch. Piece measures 12 in/30.5 cm (13.5 in/34.5 cm, 14.75 in/37.5 cm).

Cast off all sts.

SLEEVES

Place right sleeve sts on needle.

With RS facing, attach yarn.

Cast off 4 sts at the beginning of the next 2 rows. 28 sts.

Work 4 rows in seed stitch.

Cast off all sts.

Repeat for left sleeve.

Finishing

Sew sleeve seams. If there are any gaps under the arms from the sleeve join, stitch those up as well. Weave in all ends.

Block as desired

Sew on buttons opposite buttonholes.

Emily dress

When I was a little girl, I loved dresses with wide, gathered skirts that billowed out when I twirled. I called them "spinny dresses." I designed this dress for my friend Nicole's daughter Emily—a delicate and sweet girl who deserves a simple and charming dress like this one.

SIZES 0–3 (3–6, 6–12) months (shown in 6–12 months)

MATERIALS
3 x 1¾ oz balls Rowan Cashsoft DK
   (shade: Lake 543)
1 x set of US 7 circular needle
4 x safety pins
1 x stitch marker
Tapestry needle

GAUGE
22 sts and 30 rows to 4 in (10 cm) over st st
   using US 7 needles.

Work round 4 only until piece measures 7 in/18 cm (8½ in/22 cm, 10 in/26 cm) measured from tip of scallop.

Next round: * p2tog, repeat from * to end. 96 (104, 112) sts.

3–6 AND 3–6 MONTHS ONLY

Next round: k21 (23), sl sl k, k2, k2tog, k42 (46), sl sl k, k2, k2tog, k to end. 92 (100) sts.

6–12 MONTHS ONLY

Next round: k24, sl 1 k2tog psso, k2, sl 1 k2tog psso, k48, sl 1 k2tog psso, k2, sl 1 k2tog psso, k to end, 104 sts.

ALL SIZES

Next round: p to end.

Next round: k to end.

Next round: p to end.

K each round for ½ in/1 cm.

Next round: k to last 10 sts, cast off 20 sts for center back. 72 (80, 84) sts.

WORK IN SHORT ROWS

Next row: k to 1 st before end, wrap next st by slipping it onto your right needle, wrapping the yarn behind the st, and slipping the st back to left needle. Turn.

Next row: p to 1 st before end, wrap next st, turn.

Next row: k to 1 st before wrapped st, wrap next st, turn.

Next row: p to 1 st before wrapped st, wrap next st, turn.

Repeat from * until there are 6 (8, 10) wrapped sts on each side.

Next row: k to wrapped st, *pick up wrap and k wrap and st together. Repeat from * to end of row. Turn.

Pattern

CO 192 (208, 224) sts. Join to work in the round, and place marker to mark end of round.

Round 1: p to end.

Round 2: k to end.

Round 3 (scallop round): *p2, m1, k5, sl 1 k2tog psso, k5, m1, p1, repeat from * to end of round.

Round 4: p2, *k13, p3, repeat from * to last 14 sts, k13, p1.

Repeat last 2 rounds 3 (4, 5) times more.

Next row: sl 1, p to wrapped st, *pick up wrap and k wrap and st together. Repeat from * to end of row. Front of bodice measures 2.5 in/6.25 cm (3 in/7.5 cm, 3.5 in/9 cm).

Cast off all sts.

Finishing

Beginning at center back, pick up and k 92 (100, 104) sts around neckline. Join to work in the round and place marker to mark end of round.

Round 1: p to end.

Round 1: k to end.

Round 1: p to end.

Cast off 13 (15, 16) sts, k3, cast off 14 sts, k3, cast off 26 (30, 32) sts, k3, cast off 14 sts, k3, cast off 13 (15, 16) sts.

Place all 4 sets of strap sts on safety pins.

Place left front strap sts on needles.

Row 1: p1, k1, p1.

Row 2: k1, p1, k1.

Repeat these 2 rows for 7 in/18 cm (7½ in/19 cm, 8 in/20 cm). Graft strap sts to right back held sts using Kitchener stitch (see page 17).

Repeat this process for right front strap. Note that straps will cross over the back.

Weave in ends.

Block lightly so as not to stretch out ribbing.

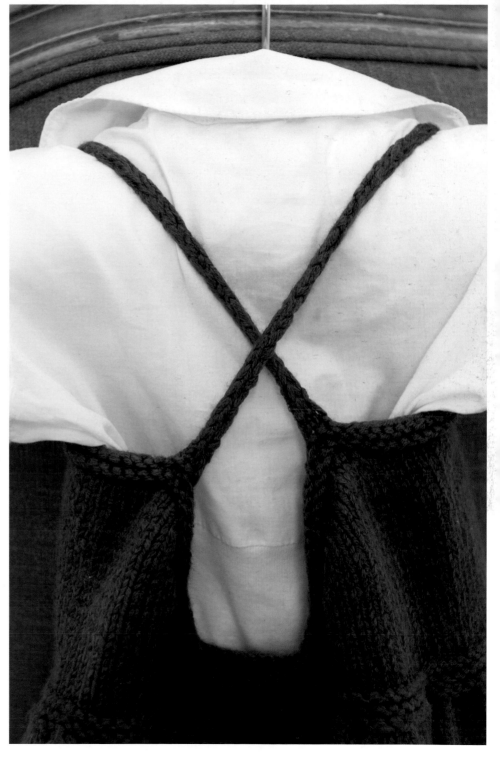

the third trimester

Impatience is the only word for this period of pregnancy, and so all of these patterns are quick to knit. While they are all simple, some have just enough complexity to provide a bit of a distraction while you wait. Maddox hat, time flies booties, and the owl and monkey pillows will help keep anxious hands occupied.

chickadee hat

My daughter Maile loves Pete Seeger's lullaby "Little Bird, Little Bird, Fly Through My Window" and we often sing it with the names of various birds inserted into the song ("Mockingbird, Mockingbird, fly through my window" or "Dodo Bird, Dodo Bird, fly through my window" and so on). But our favorite is the chickadee. The hat fits tightly so the circumference listed here is smaller than on page 10.

SIZES 0–6 months (14⅕ in / 36 cm circumference), 6–12 months (15¾ in / 40 cm circumference) (shown in 6–12 months).

MATERIALS
MC: 1 × 1¾ oz ball Debbie Bliss Baby Cashmerino (shade: 100 White) for MC
CC: 1 × 1¾ oz ball Debbie Bliss Baby Cashmerino (shade: 001 Yellow) for CC
1 × set of US 2 double-pointed needles
1 × set of US 2 circular needles
2 × black 8 mm buttons
Tapestry needle and needle and thread

GAUGE
28 sts and 30 rows to 4 in (10 cm) over st st using US 2 needles.

Pattern

EAR FLAPS (MAKE 2)

Using dpns and MC, CO 3 sts. Work i-cord (see page 14) for 9 in (22 cm).

Row 1: (RS): k1, m1, k1, m1, k1. 5 sts.

Row 2: k to end.

Row 3: k1, m1, k to last st, m1, k1. 7 sts.

Row 4: k to end.

Row 5: k1, m1, k to last st, m1, k1. 9 sts.

Row 6: k to end.

*Row 7: k1, m1, k to last st, m1, k1. 11 sts.

Row 8: k4, p to last 4 sts, end k4.

Repeat from * until there are 21 (23) sts.

Break yarn, leave sts on dpn and set aside.

BILL

Using dpns and CC, CO 3 sts.

Row 1: (WS): k to end.

Row 2: k1, m1, k to last st, m1, k1. 5 sts.

Row 3: k to end.

Row 4: k1, m1, k to last st, m1, k1. 7 sts.

Row 5: k to end.

Row 6: k1, m1, k to last st, m1, k1. 9 sts.

Row 7: k to end. 9 sts.

Row 8: k1, m1, k to last st, m1, k1. 11 sts.

*Row 9: k4, p to last 4 sts, k4.

Row 10: k1, m1, k to last st, m1, k1. 13 sts.

Repeat from * until there are 17 sts.

Next row: k4, p to last 4 sts, k4.

Break yarn. Leave sts on dpn and set aside.

BRIM

Using circular needle and MC, k across sts of first earflap. Using the cable cast-on method (see page 13), CO 25 (29) sts, k across second earflap, cable cast-on 8 (10) sts, k across bill, cable cast-on 8 (10) sts. Join to work in the round. 100 (112) sts. (Note: Cable cast-on sts often twist, so take care to ensure sts are straight when joining sts to work in the round.)

Round 1: (RS): p3, k15 (17), p31 (35), k15 (17), p14 (16), k11, p11 (13).

Round 2: k to end.

Round 3: p2, k17 (19), p29 (33), k17 (19), p12 (14), k13, p10 (12).

Round 4: k to end.

Round 5: p1, k19 (21), p27 (31), k19 (21), p10 (12), k15, p9 (11).

Round 6: k to end.

Work straight in st st until hat measures 4 in (10 cm) from cable cast-on edge.

CROWN

Next round: *k8 (12), k2tog, repeat from * to end. 90 (104) sts.

Next round: k to end.

Next round: *k7 (11), k2tog, repeat from * to end. 80 (96) sts.

Next round: k to end.

Next round: *k6 (10), k2tog, repeat from * to end. 70 (88) sts.

Next round: k to end.

Next round: *5 (9), k2tog, repeat from * to end. 60 (80) sts.

Next round: k to end.

Next round: *k4 (8), k2tog, repeat from * to end. 50 (72) sts.

Next round: k to end.

Next round: *k3 (7), k2tog, repeat from * end. 40 (64) sts.

Next round: k to end.

Next round: *k2 (6), k2tog, repeat from * end. 30 (56) sts.

LARGE SIZE ONLY

Next round: k to end.

Next round: *k5, k2tog, repeat from * to end. 48 sts.

Next round: k to end.

Next round: *k4, k2tog, repeat from * to end. 40 sts.

Next round: *k3, k2tog, repeat from * to end. 32 sts.

Next round: *k2, k2tog, repeat from * to end. 24 sts.

ALL SIZES

Next round: *k1, k2tog, repeat from * to end. 20 (16) sts.

Next round: *k2tog, repeat from * to end. 10 (8) sts.

Break yarn, leaving a long tail. Draw tail through remaining sts and pull tight, closing the hole. Weave in ends, checking to tighten any gaps at the cable cast-on edge.

Finishing
Sew buttons as pictured.

To make a pom-pom, cut a rectangular piece of cardboard to about 1 in (3 cm) wide and 1½ in (4 cm) long. Wind both MC and CC around the cardboard many times – more really is more here. Break yarn. Using MC insert your tapestry needle under your windings against the cardboard. Cinch a very tight knot around the windings (this knot will hold your pom-pom together, so make sure it is firm), and break your yarn, leaving a long tail. Turn the cardboard over and cut your yarn on the opposite side from where you've tied your knot. The yarn will pouf, but it will pouf more as you trim it, using a pair of very sharp scissors wisely to create a ball (I find I always make a big mess doing this). Sew the pom-pom onto the top of the hat using the long tail.

time flies booties

These precious booties are perfect for delicate little baby feet, and they have an old-fashioned simplicity that is sure to warm the heart.

SIZE 0–3 months

MATERIALS
1 x 1¾ oz ball Debbie Bliss Baby Cashmerino (shade: 001 Yellow)
1 x set of US 2 double-pointed needles
2 x 8 mm buttons
Tapestry needle
Needle and thread

GAUGE
26 sts and 37 rows to 4 in (10 cm) over st st using US 2 needles.

Pattern

RIGHT BOOTIE

CO 40 sts, leaving a long tail. Divide sts evenly onto dpns and join to work in the round. P 1 round.

Round 1: RS: p to end.

Round 2: k1, m1, k18, m1, k2, m1, k18, m1, k1. 44 sts.

Round 3: p to end.

Round 4: k2, m1, k18, m1, k4, m1, k18, m1, k2. 48 sts.

Round 5: p to end.

Round 6: k3, m1, k18, m1, k6, m1, k18, m1, k3. 52 sts.

Round 7: p to end.

Round 8: k4, m1, k18, m1, k8, m1, k18, m1, k4. 56 sts.

Round 9: p to end.

Round 10: k to end.

Round 11: p to end.

Rounds 12–17: k to end.

Round 18: k20, (sl sl k) × 4, (k2tog) × 4, k20. 48 sts.

Round 19: k20, (yf, k2tog) × 4, k20.

Round 20: k to end.

Round 21: k18, (sl sl k) × 3, (k2tog) × 3, k18. 42 sts.

Round 22: k10, cast off 22 sts, k10.

RIGHT BOOTIE STRAP

Next row: k10, so that all 20 remaining sts are on one dpn, ready to work in rows, CO 14 sts using the backward-loop cast-on method (see page 13). 34 sts.

Next row: k to end.

Next row: k to last 3 sts, k2tog, yf, k1.

Next row: k to end.

Cast off all sts knitwise.

LEFT BOOTIE

Work as for right bootie until you have completed round 22, then continue as follows:

LEFT BOOTIE STRAP

Next row: k10, so that all 20 remaining sts are on one dpn, ready to work in rows.

Next row: p20, CO 14 sts using the backward-loop cast-on method. 34 sts.

Next row: p to end.

Next row: p to last 3 sts, p2tog, yo, p1.

Next row: p to end.

Cast off all sts purlwise.

Finishing

Sew up seam on sole of booties using the CO tail. Weave in ends of straps. Sew on buttons opposite buttonhole.

Block as follows: soak the bootie in warm water to relax the sts, then shape with your hands. You can stuff it lightly with absorbent cotton balls or a small washcloth to help it keep its shape if you desire. Leave to dry.

burp cloths

These three designs are practical, soften with use (and, oh, the use they will get!) and are mindless enough knitting to help get you through those last few weeks before the birth. I love the yarn, both for its subtle simplicity of color, and because it provides a completely natural surface against which my daughter can rest her face. Designate a ball to each cloth, but match color to texture as you wish.

SIZE One size

MATERIALS
1 × 1¾ oz ball Rowan Belle Organic DK by
   Amy Butler Cotton DK (shade: 009 Hibiscus)
1 × 1¾ oz ball Rowan Belle Organic DK by
   Amy Butler Cotton DK (shade: 015 slate)
1 × 1¾ oz ball Rowan Belle Organic DK by
   Amy Butler Cotton DK shade (017 zinc)
1 × pair of US 8 needles
Tapestry needle

GAUGE
23 sts and 28 rows to 4 in (10 cm) over st st.
   using US 8 needles.

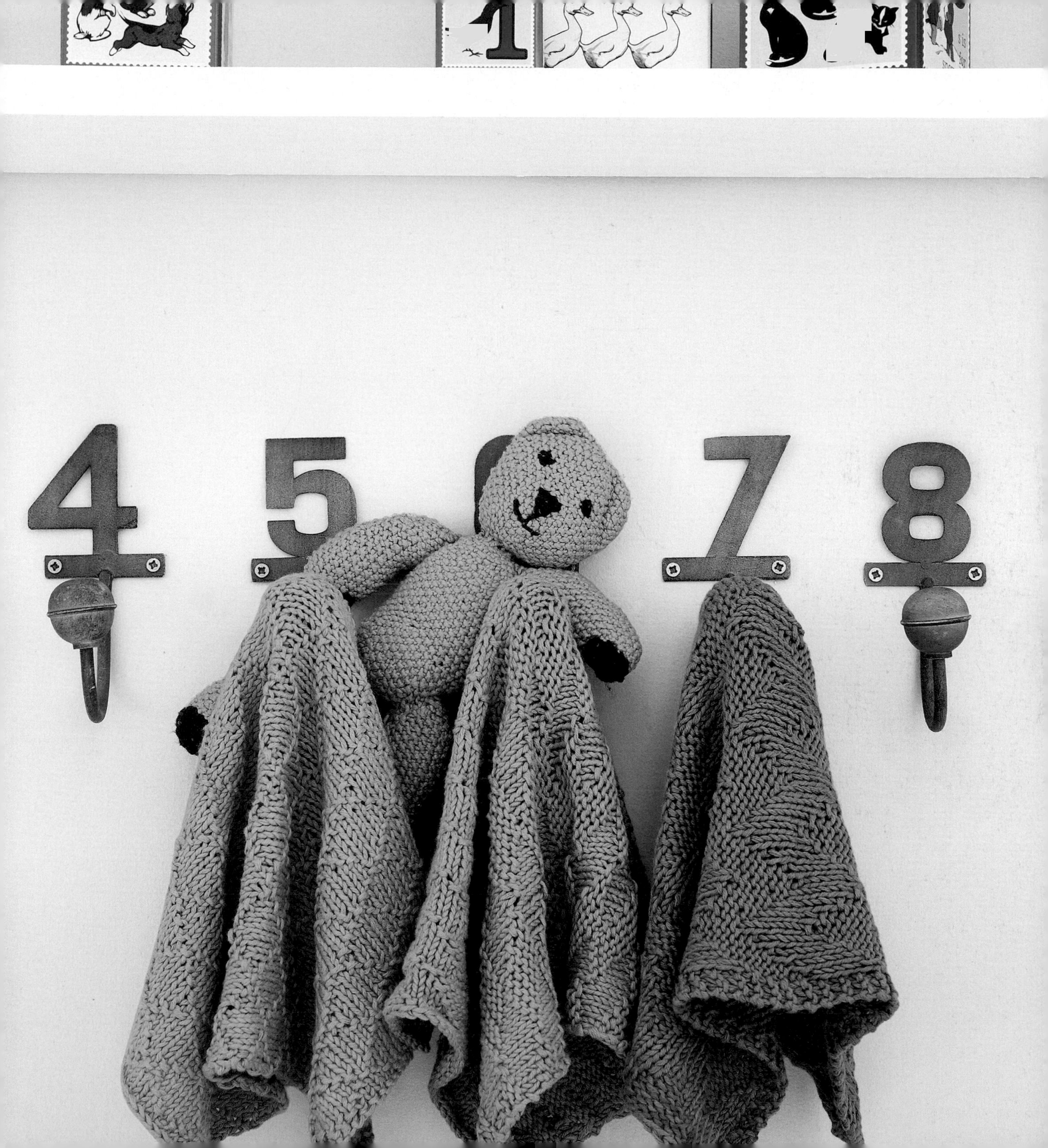
4
5
7
8

Diamond brocade cloth

CO 49 sts.

Row 1: k4, *p1, k7, repeat from * to last 5 sts, p1, k4.

Row 2: p3, *k1, p1, k1, p5, repeat from * to last 6 sts, k1, p1, k1, p3.

Row 3: k2, *p1, k3, repeat from * to last 3 sts, p1, k2.

Row 4: p1, *k1, p5, k1, p1, repeat from * to end.

Row 5: *k1, k7, repeat from * to last st, p1.

Row 6: as row 4.

Row 7: as row 3.

Row 8: as row 2.

Repeat these 8 rows until piece measures approximately 16 in (40 cm), ending with row 1 or 5.

Cast off all sts.

Parallelogram check cloth

CO 50 sts.

Row 1: *k5, p5, repeat from * to end.

Row 2: k4, *p5, k5, repeat from * to last 6 sts, p5, k1.

Row 3: p2, *k5, p5, repeat from * to last 8 sts, k5, p3.

Row 4: k2, *p5, k5, repeat from * to last 8 sts, p5, k3.

Row 5: p4, *k5, p5, repeat from * to last 6 sts, k5, p1.

Row 6: *p5, k5, repeat from * to end.

Repeat these 6 rows until piece measures approximately 16 in (40 cm), ending with row 6.

Cast off all sts.

Chevron cloth

CO 47 sts.

Row 1: k4, *p7, k1, repeat from * to last 3 sts, k3.

Row 2: k3, p1, *k7, p1, repeat from * to last 3 sts, k3

Row 3: k5, *p5, k3, repeat from * to last 10 sts, p5, k5.

Row 4: k3, p2, *k5, p3, repeat from * to last 10 sts, k5, p2, k3.

Row 5: k6, *p3, k5, repeat from * to last 9 sts, p3, k6.

Row 6: k3, p3, *k3, p5, repeat from * to last 9 sts, k3, p3, k3.

Row 7: k7, *p1, k7, repeat from * to last 8 sts, p1, k7.

Row 8: k3, p4, *k1, p7, repeat from * to last 8 sts, k1, p4, k3.

Row 9: as row 2.

Row 10: as row 1.

Row 11: as row 4.

Row 12: as row 3.

Row 13: as row 6.

Row 14: as row 5.

Row 15: as row 8.

Row 16: as row 7.

Repeat these 16 rows until piece measures approximately 16 in (40 cm), ending with row 8 or row 16.

Cast off all sts.

Finishing

Weave in ends. Soak cloth in lukewarm water to relax sts. Lay flat to dry, stretching to desired width and length.

bib

*No mother needs to be told how entirely
practical it is to have a few good bibs
on hand. This classic bib pattern
is very quick work.*

SIZE 5in / 13cm x 6in / 15cm

MATERIALS
1 x 1¾ oz ball Rowan Belle Organic DK by
  Amy Butler (shade: 009 Hibiscus) for MC
1 x 1¾ oz ball Rowan Belle Organic DK by
  Amy Butler (shade: 015 Slate) for CC
1 pair of US 5 needles
1 set of US 4 circular needles
1 set of US 4 double-pointed needles (optional)

GAUGE
22.5 sts and 31 rows to 4 in (10 cm) over st st
  using US 5 needles.

Pattern

BIB

Using US 5 needles and MC, CO 30 sts.

Row 1 (WS): *p to end.

Row 2: k2, m1, k to last 2 sts, m1, k2.

Repeat from * until you have 40 sts.

Work straight in st st until piece measures 6 in (15 cm), ending with a WS row.

Next row: k10, cast off 20, k10.

RIGHT NECKLINE

Leaving sts for left neckline on the needle, begin to work right neckline.

Next row: p to last 3 sts, p2togtbl, p1. 9 sts.

*Next row: k to end.

Next row: p to last 3 sts, p2togtbl, p1. 9 sts.

Repeat from * until 3 sts remain.

Next row: k to end.

Next row: p2togtbl, p1.

Next row: k2tog.

Break yarn and draw tail through remaining st.

Rejoin yarn to remaining stitches and work left neckline as for right, reversing all shaping.

Finishing

BIB EDGING

Weave in ends.

With RS facing and using circular needles and CC, pick up and k 110 sts around outside edge of bib (not including neckline).

Next row: k to end.

CO 3sts using cable cast-on method (see page 13) onto left needle.

*Next row: k2, p2tog, slip sts onto left needle, pulling yarn around and across **back** of sts. Repeat from * across until 3 sts remain. Break yarn. Draw tail through remaining 3 sts and pull tight.

With RS facing, pick up, and using circular needle and CC pick up and k40 sts around neckline.

Next row: k to end.

Work edging as for outside edge of bib.

RIGHT NECKLINE CORD

Using dpns or circular needles and CC, with RS facing, pick up and k 2 sts from uppermost edge of neckline i-cord, 1 st from the space where the outer-edge i-cord and neckline I-cords meet, and 2 sts from edge of outer-edge i-cord (5 sts).

Slide sts to other end of right needle, bring yarn around back of sts, and k2tog, k1, k2tog (3 sts).

Work i-cord (see page 14) for 11⅘ in (30 cm). Break yarn and draw it through remaining sts.

Repeat for left neckline.

Weave in ends. Block as desired.

summer bucket hat

It took Maile a long time to agree to wear a hat and, bizarrely, it was the summertime that got her to change her mind. She doesn't care if her ears get cold, but she can't bear the sun being in her eyes. This bucket-style cotton hat has just enough of a brim to shade the eyes without blocking the view, and the slightly elasticized yarn helps it to stay on. The hat fits tightly so the circumference listed here is smaller than on page 10.

SIZES 0–6 months (14½ in / 37 cm circumference) and 6–12 months (15¾ in / 40 cm circumference) (shown in 6–12 months).

MATERIALS
1 × 1¾ oz ball Rowan All Seasons Cotton (shade: 191 Jersey)
1 × set of US 5 circular needles
1 × set of US 7 circular needles
1 × set of US 7 double-pointed needles
Tapestry needle

GAUGE
18 sts and 28.5 rows to 4 in (10 cm) over st st using US 5 needles
17 sts and 27 rows to 4 in (10 cm) over st st using US 7 needles.

Pattern

BRIM

Using US 5 circular needles, CO 112 sts. Join to work in the round.

Round 1: p to end.

Round 2: *k12, k2tog, repeat from * to end. 104 sts.

Round 3: p to end.

Round 4: *k11, k2tog, repeat from * to end. 96 sts.

Round 5: p to end.

Round 6: *k10, k2tog, repeat from * to end. 88 sts.

Round 7: p to end.

Round 8: *k9, k2tog, repeat from * to end. 80 sts.

Round 9: p to end.

Round 10: *k8, k2tog, repeat from * to end. 72 sts.

Round 11: p to end.

Change to US 7 circular needles.

0–3 MONTHS ONLY
Next round: (k7, k2tog) × 8. 64 sts.

6–12 MONTHS ONLY
Next round: (k16, k2tog) × 4. 68 sts.

ALL SIZES
Work straight in st st until st st section measures 3 in/ 8 cm (3½ in/9 cm).

6–12 MONTHS ONLY
Next round: (k32, k2tog) × 2. 66 sts.

CROWN

ALL SIZES
Begin decreases for crown, changing to dpns when necessary.

Next round: *k6 (9), k2tog, repeat from * to end. 56 (60) sts.

Next round: k to end.

Next round: *k5 (8), k2tog, repeat from * to end. 48 (54) sts.

Next round: k to end.

Next round: *k4 (7), k2tog, repeat from * to end. 40 (48) sts.

Next round: k to end.

Next round: *k3 (6), k2tog, repeat from * to end. 32 (42) sts.

Next round: k to end.

Next round: *k2 (5), k2tog, repeat from * to end.

Next round: k to end.

Next round: *k1 (4), k2tog, repeat from * to end. 16 (30) sts.

Next round: k to end.

Next round: *k0 (3), k2tog, repeat from * to end. 8 (24) sts.

6—12 MONTHS ONLYY
Next round: *k2, (k2tog), repeat from * to end. 18 sts.

Next round: *k1, (k2tog), repeat from * to end. 12 sts.

Finishing

ALL SIZES
Break yarn, leaving a long tail. Pull it through remaining sts, and pull tight, closing the hole. Weave in ends.

button bag

Button bags are traditional toys for older children, who love to pack and unpack oversized buttons. As buttons may present a hazard, make sure they are securely sewn on. The bag is knitted from the inside out, and this kind of slipped-stitch double-knitting allows you to knit in the round with a pair of straight needles! Decorate with buttons, bells or whatever you have handy. The buttonhole is intentionally loose for tiny fingers to practise on.

SIZES 4.7 in/12cm x 6.2 in/16 cm

MATERIALS
1 x 1¾ oz ball Mirasol Sampa 100% Organic
   Naturally Dyed Cotton Yarn
1 x pair of US 6 needles
Stitch holder
Tapestry needle
Assorted buttons, including a 27 mm button
Needle and thread

GAUGE
20 sts and 28 rows to 4 in (10 cm) over st st
   using US 6 needles.

Pattern

CO 66 sts

Row 1 (RS): k1, sl 1 purlwise, repeat from * to end.

Repeat this row until piece measures 5 in (12 cm), ending on an even row.

Next row: sl 1 st onto stitch holder, sl next st onto your free needle. Repeat until you have 33 sts on needle and 33 sts on holder.

Row 1 (RS): p2, k29, p2.

Row 2: k2, p29, k2.

Repeat last 2 rows for 3 in (7 cm), ending with a WS row.

Buttonhole row: p2, k13, cast off 3 sts, k13, p2.

Next row: k2, p13, CO 3 sts using the backward-loop cast-on method (see page 13), p13, k2

Repeat rows 1 and 2 for 1 in (3 cm), ending with a WS row.

Next row: p to end.

Next row: k to end.

Cast off all sts.

Place stitches on holder back on to needle. Attach yarn and cast off all sts loosely.

Finishing

Weave in ends.

Press lightly, creating creases at edges of bag to help maintain its rectangular shape. Sew 27 mm button behind its buttonhole. Sew various buttons on exterior of bag.

Maddox hat

I love Seattle—it's a great town, it is full of arty people and has a very friendly vibe. But my friend Laura lived there briefly and loathed it! Her son, Maddox, was a Seattle resident for all of three months, but he was born there, so this warm, funky little hat is for him, in honor of the Seattle blood that's in him somewhere. The hat fits tightly so the circumference listed here is smaller than on page 10.

SIZES 0–6 months (15 in/38 cm circumference) and 6–12 months (15¾ in/40 cm circumference) (shown in 0–6 months)

MATERIALS
1 skein Manos Del Uruguay Wool Classica (shade: 55 Olive)
1 × set of US 9 double-pointed needles
1 × set of US 9 circular needles
1 × 19 mm button
3 × safety pins
Tapestry needle
Needle and thread

GAUGE
16 sts and 22.5 rows to 4 in (10 cm) over st st using US 9 needles.

Pattern

Using circular needles, CO 60 (64) sts and join to work in the round.

Work in st st for 4 rounds.

Next round: *k2tog, yf, repeat from * to end.

Work in st st for 4 rounds.

Next round: *take a dpn and slide it through the CO loop that corresponds with the next live st on your circular needle. Fold the cuff along the fifth row of knitting (the row with the yarn-forwards). K1 st from working needle together with the corresponding st on your dpn, repeat from * to end. Pin a safety pin at the hem at the beginning of the round to mark the center back.

Work straight in st st until piece measures 4 in/10 cm (4½ in/11 cm).

CROWN

ALL SIZES

Begin decreases for crown, changing to dpns when necessary.

Next round: *k8 (6), k2tog, repeat from * to end. 54 (56) sts.

Next round: k to end.

Next round: *k7 (5), k2tog, repeat from * to end. 48 sts.

Next round: k to end.

Next round: *k6 (4), k2tog, repeat from * to end. 42 (40) sts.

Next round: k to end.

Next round: *k5 (3), k2tog, repeat from * to end. 36 (32) sts.

Next round: k to end.

Next round: *k4 (2), k2tog, repeat from * to end. 30 (24) sts.

Next round: k to end.

Next round: *k3 (1), k2tog, repeat from * to end. 24 (16) sts.

0–3 MONTHS ONLY
Next round: *k2, k2tog, repeat from * to end. 18 sts.

Next round: *k1 k2tog, repeat from * to end. 12 sts.

ALL SIZES
Next round: *k2tog, repeat from * to end. 6 (8) sts.

Break yarn, leaving a long tail. Draw tail through remaining sts and pull tight, closing the hole.

Finishing
Weave in ends.

RIGHT EAR FLAP
Place a second safety pin 2½ (6 cm) in to the right of the pin marking the center back. Starting at this second pin, using dnps, fold up cuff and pick up and k 11 (13) sts from the first WS row of the body of the hat, just above the cuff.

Next row: k to end.

Work in st st until piece measures 2 in (5 cm).

Decrease 1 st at each end of next and every other row until 5 sts remain.

Work even in garter stitch until piece measures 3½ in (9 cm).

Next row: k2, yf, k2tog, k1.

K 2 rows.

Cast off all sts.

LEFT EARFLAP
Place a third safety pin 2½ in (6 cm) to the left of the center back pin. Pick up 11 (13) sts from the first WS row of the body of the hat, just above the cuff and work as for right earflap until 5 sts remain.

Work straight in garter stitch for ¾ in (2 cm).

Cast off all sts.

Sew button opposite buttonhole.

Weave in ends.

owl & monkey pillows

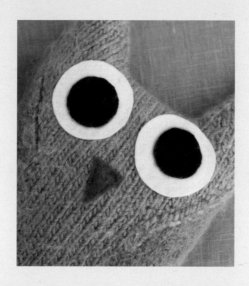

My daughter Maile has a split personality. Sometimes she is goofy and rambunctious and generally a maniac, while other times she is solemn and curious. These pillows were made to represent two of the many seemingly opposing sides children can show.

OWL MATERIALS

1 × 3½ oz ball Rowan Cocoon (shade: 825 Clay) for MC
1 ball Rowan Cocoon (shade: 816 Kiwi) for CC
1 × pair of US 10 needles
Small amounts of brown, white and yellow felt
Tapestry needle and needle and thread
Stuffing

MONKEY MATERIALS

1 × 3½ oz ball Rowan Cocoon (shade: 815 Amber) for MC
1 ball Rowan Cocoon (shade: 806 Frost) for CC
1 × pair of US 10 needles
Small amounts of brown felt

GAUGE

15.5 sts and 22.5 rows to 4 in (10 cm) over st st using US 10 needles.

Patterns
Owl
BACK
Using MC, CO 15 sts.

Row 1 (WS): p to end.

Row 2: k2, m1, k to last 2 sts, m1, k2. 17 sts.

Repeat last 2 rows 3 times more. 23 sts.

*Next row: p to end

Next row: k to end.

Next row: p1, m1, p to last st, m1, p1. 25 sts.

Next row: k to end.

Next row: p to end.

Next row: k1, m1, k to last st, m1, k1. 27 sts.

Repeat from * once more. 31 sts.

Work straight in st st until piece measures 11 in (28 cm), ending with a RS row.

Next row: p11, cast off 9 sts purlwise, p11.

LEFT HORN
Next row: Leaving the stitches for the right horn on the needle, k to 4 sts before cast-off section, k2tog, k2. 10 sts.

**Next row: p to end.

Next row: k to last 4 sts, k2tog, k2. 9 sts.

Repeat from ** until 4 sts remain.

Next row: p to end.

Next row: k1, k2tog, k1. 3 sts.

Cast off remaining 3 sts purlwise.

RIGHT HORN
Attach yarn with the RS facing.

Next row: k2, sl sl k, k to end. 10 sts.

***Next row: p to end.

Next row: k2, sl sl k, k to end. 9 sts.

Repeat from *** until 4 sts remain.

Next row: p to end.

Next row: k1, sl sl k, k1. 3 sts.

Cast off remaining 3 sts purlwise.

FRONT
Divide CC into 2 balls.

Using MC, CO 15 sts.

Row 1: p to end.

Row 2: k2, m1, k to last st, m1, k2. 17 sts.

Row 3: Attach first ball of CC, p1 with CC, p1 with CC and MC held together, p with MC to last 2 sts, attach second ball of CC, p1 with CC and MC held together, p1 with CC.

Row 4: k1 with CC, m1 in CC, k1 with CC and MC held together, k with MC to last 2 sts, k1 in CC and MC held together, m1 in CC, k1 in CC. 19 sts.

Row 5: p2 with CC, p1 with CC and MC held together, p with MC to last 3 sts, p1 with CC and MC held together, p2 with CC.

Row 6: k2 with CC, m1 with CC, k1 with CC and MC

held together, k with MC to last 3 sts, k1 with CC and MC held together, m1 in CC, k2 in CC. 21 sts.

Row 7: p3 with CC, p1 with CC and MC held together, p with MC to last 4 sts, p1 with CC and MC held together, p3 with CC.

Row 8: k2 with CC, m1 with CC, k1 in CC, k1 in CC and MC held together, k with MC to last 4 sts, k1 with CC and MC held together, k1 with CC, m1 in CC, k2 in CC. 23 sts.

Work 2 rows straight using colors as established in the previous row.

Next row (WS): p2 with CC, m1 with CC, p2 with CC, p1 with CC and MC held together, p with MC to last 5 sts, p1 with CC and MC, p2 with CC, m1 with CC, p2 with CC. 25 sts.

Work 2 rows straight using colors as set by previous row.

Next row (RS): k2 with CC, m1 with CC, k3 with CC, k1 with CC and MC held together, k with MC to last 6 sts, k1 with CC and MC held together, k3 with CC, m1 with CC, k2 with CC. 27 sts.

Work 2 rows straight using colors as set by previous row.

Next row (WS): p2 with CC, m1 with CC, p4 with CC, p1 with CC and MC held together, p with MC to last 7 sts, p1 with CC and MC held together, p4 with CC, m1 with CC, p2 with CC. 29 sts.

Work 2 rows straight using colors as set by previous row.

Next row (RS): k2 with CC, m1 with CC, k5 with CC, k1

with CC and MC held together, k with MC to last 8 sts, k1 with CC and MC, k5 with CC, m1 with CC, k2 with CC. 31 sts.

Work straight, using colors as set by previous row, until piece measures 7 in, ending with a WS row.

Next row (RS): k7 with CC, k2tog with CC and MC held together, m1 with MC, k with MC to last 9 sts, m1 with MC, sl sl k with CC and MC held together, k7 with CC.

Next row: p to end, using colors as set in the previous row.

Next row: k6 with CC, k2tog with CC and MC held together, m1 with MC, k with MC to last 8 sts, m1 with MC, sl sl k with CC and MC held together, k6 with CC.

Next row: p to end, using colors as set in the previous row.

Next row: k5 with CC, k2tog with CC and MC held together, m1 with MC, k with MC to last 7 sts, m1 with MC, sl sl k with CC and MC held together, k5 with CC.

Next row: p to end, using colors as set in the previous row.

Next row: k4 with CC, k2tog with CC and MC held together, m1 with MC, k with MC to last 6 sts, m1 with MC, sl sl k with CC and MC held together, k4 with CC.

Next row: p to end, using colors as set in the previous row.

Next row: k3 with CC, k2tog with CC and MC held together, m1 with MC, k with MC to last 5 sts, m1 with MC, sl sl k with CC & MC, k3 with CC.

Next row: p to end, using colors as set in the previous row.

Next row: k2 with CC, k2tog with CC and MC held together, m1 with MC, k with MC to last 4 sts, m1 with MC, sl sl k with CC and MC held together, k2 with CC.

Next row: p to end, using colors as set in the previous row.

Next row: k1 with CC, k2tog with CC and MC held together, m1 with MC, k with MC to last 3 sts, m1 with MC, sl sl k with CC and MC held together, k1 with CC.

Next row: p to end, using colors as set in the previous row.

Next row: k2tog with CC and MC held together, m1 with MC, k with MC to last 2 sts, m1 with MC, sl sl k with CC and MC held together.

Break off CC.

Work straight in MC only until piece measures 11 in (28 cm), ending with a WS row.

Work horns as for back.

Finishing

Weave in ends. Sew front and back together using MC, leaving top between horns open for stuffing.

Felt by tossing the owl into the washing machine with a pair of old jeans. Run it on a warm setting, fairly gentle, checking it often. (A hot wash will felt faster, but you'll have less control, and will need to check it a lot more frequently. Washing machines differ, so trust your eyes and your instincts – you're looking for a fabric that is stiff enough to hold its shape, but not so stiff that the shape becomes distorted. I'd wait until the stitches are blurred almost completely, but not quite. If you're making both pillows, felt them at the same time).

Sew on eyes and beak as pictured. Stuff very lightly, as we're making pillows, not owl-shaped balls. Keep it as flat as you can. Sew up opening.

Monkey
BACK
Using MC, CO 20 sts.

*Row 1 (WS): p to end.

Row 2: k2, m1, k to last 2 sts, m1, k2. 22 sts.

Repeat from * until there are 30 sts.

Next row: p to end.

Next row: k to end.

Next row: p2, m1p, p to last 2 sts, m1p, p2. 32 sts.

Next row: k to end.

Next row: p to end.

Next row: k2, m1, k to last 2 sts, m1, k2. 34 sts.

**Next row: p to end.

Next row: k to end.

Next row: p to end.

Next row: k2, m1, k to last 2 sts, m1, k2. 36 sts.

Repeat from ** until there are 40 sts.

Work 5 rows straight in st st.

Next row: k2, sl sl k, k to last 4 sts, k2tog, k2. 38 sts.

***Next row: p to end.

Next row: k to end.

Next row: p to end.

Next row: k2, sl sl k, k to last 4 sts, k2tog, k2. 36 sts.

Repeat from *** until 34 sts remain.

Next row: p to end.

Next row: k to end.

Next row: p to end.

Next row: k2, sl sl k, k to last 4 sts, k2tog, k2. 32 sts.

Next row: p to end.

Next row: k to end.

Next row: p2, p2tog, p to last 4 sts, p2togtbl, p4. 30 sts.

Next row: k to end.

Next row: p to end.

Next row: k2, sl sl k, k to last 4 sts, k2tog, k2. 28 sts.

*****Next row:* p to end.

Next row: k2, sl sl k, k to last 4 sts, k2tog, k2. 26 sts.

Repeat from **** until 20 sts remain.

Next row: p to end.

Cast off all sts.

FRONT

Wind remaining MC into 2 balls.

Using 1 ball of MC, CO 20 sts.

Row 1 (WS): p to end.

Row 2: k2, m1, k to last 2 sts, m1, k2. 22 sts.

Repeat from * once more. 24 sts.

Next row: p to end.

Next row: k2, m1, k2, drop first ball of MC and attach CC and second ball of MC, k with CC and second ball of MC held together to last 4 sts, k2 with second ball of MC, m1 with MC, k2 with MC. 26 sts.

Next row: p4 with MC, p1 with CC and MC held together, p with CC to last 5 sts, p1 with CC and MC held together, p4 with MC.

Next row: k2 with MC, m1 with MC, k1 with MC, k2tog with CC and MC held together, m1 with CC, k16 with CC, m1 with CC, sl sl k with CC and MC held together, k1 with MC, m1 with MC, k2 with MC. 28 sts.

Next row: p to end, using colors as set in the previous row.

Next row: k2 with MC, m1 with MC, k1 with MC, k2tog with CC and MC held together, m1 with CC, k18 with CC, m1 with CC, sl sl k with CC & MC, k1 with MC, m1 with MC, k2 with MC. 30 sts.

Next row: p to end, using colors as set in the previous row.

Next row: k to end, using colors as set in the previous row.

Next row: p2 with MC, m1p with MC, p1 with MC, p2togtbl with CC and MC held together, m1p with CC, k20 with CC, m1p with CC, p2tog with CC and MC held together, p1 with MC, m1p with MC, p1 with MC. 32 sts.

Next row: k to end, using colors as set in the previous row.

Next row: p to end, using colors as set in the previous row.

Next row: k2 with MC, m1 with MC, k1 with MC, k2tog with CC and MC held together, m1 with CC, k22 with CC, m1 with CC, sl sl k with CC and MC held together, k1 with MC, m1 with MC, k2 with MC. 34 sts.

**Next row:* p to end, using colors as set in the previous row.

Next row: k to end, using colors as set in the previous row.

Next row: p to end, using colors as set in the previous row.

Next row: k2 with MC, m1 with MC, k1 with MC, k2tog with CC and MC held together, m1 with CC, k with CC to end of CC section, m1 in CC, sl sl k in CC and MC held together, k1 with MC, m1 with MC, k2 with MC. 36 sts.

Repeat from ** until there are 40 sts.

Work 5 rows straight using colors as set in the previous row.

Next row: k2 with MC, sl sl k with MC, m1 with MC, sl sl k with CC and MC held together, k28 with CC, k2tog with CC and MC held together, m1 with MC, k2tog with MC, k2 with MC. 40 sts.

Next row: p4, m1 with MC, p2tog with CC and MC held together, p26 with CC, p2togtbl with CC and MC held together, m1 with MC, p4 with MC.

Next row: k5, m1 with MC, sl sl k with CC and MC held together, k24 with CC, k2tog with CC and MC held together, m1 with MC, k5 with MC.

Next row: p6, m1 with MC, p2tog with CC and MC held together, p22 with CC, p2togtbl with CC and MC held together, m1, p6 in MC.

Next row: k2 with MC, sl sl k with MC, k3 with MC, m1 with MC, sl sl k with CC and MC held together, k20 with CC, k2tog with CC and MC held together, m1 with MC, k3 with MC, k2tog with MC, k2 with MC MC. 38 sts.

Work 3 rows straight using colors as set in the previous row.

Next row: k2 with MC, sl sl k with MC, k3 with MC, m1 with MC, sl sl k with CC and MC held together, k18 with CC, k2tog with CC and MC held together, m1 with MC, k3 with MC, k2tog with MC, k2 with MC. 36 sts.

Work 3 rows straight using colors as set in the previous row.

Next row: k2 with MC, sl sl k with MC, k3 with MC, k1 with CC and MC held together, k18 with CC, k1 with CC and MC held together, k3 with MC, k2tog with MC, k2 with MC. 34 sts.

Work 2 rows straight using colors as set in the previous row.

Next row: p2 with MC, p2tog with MC, p2 with MC, p1 with CC and MC held together, p18 with CC, p1 with CC and MC held together, p2 with MC, p2togtbl with MC, p2 with MC. 32 sts.

Work 2 rows straight using colors as set in the previous row.

Next row: k2 with MC, sl sl k with MC, k1 with MC, k1 with CC and MC held together, k18 with CC, k1 with CC and MC held together, k1 with MC, k2tog with MC, k2 with MC. 30 sts.

Work 1 row straight using colors as set in the previous row.

Next row: k2 with MC, sl sl k with MC, m1 with MC, sl sl k with CC and MC held together, k16 with CC, k2tog with CC and MC held together, m1 with MC, k2tog with MC, k2 with MC. 28 sts.

Next row: p4 with MC m1 with MC, p2tog with CC and MC held together, p14 with CC, p2togtbl with CC and MC held together, m1 with MC, p4 with MC.

Next row: k2 with MC, sl sl k with MC, k2 with MC, m1 with MC, sl sl k with CC and MC held together, k12 with CC, k2tog in CC and MC held together, m1 with MC, k2 with MC, k2tog with MC, k2 with MC. 26 sts.

Next row: p5 with MC, m1 with MC, p2tog with CC and MC held together, p10 with CC and MC held together, p2togtbl with CC and MC held together, m1 with MC, p5 with MC.

Break CC and second ball of MC.

Next row: Using MC only, k2, sl sl k, k to last 4 sts, k2tog, k2. 24 sts.

***Next row:* p to end.

Next row: k2, sl sl k, k to last 4 sts, k2tog, k2. 22 sts.

Repeat from *** until 20 sts remain.

Next row: p to end.

Cast off all sts.

Weave in ends.

Sew front and back together using MC, leaving top cast-off section open for stuffing.

EARS

Using MC, with RS facing, pick up and k 12 sts above the monkey's cheekbone as pictured.

K 5 rows.

*Next row (1): k1, sl sl k, k to last 3 sts, k2tog, k1. 10 sts.

Next row: k to end.

Repeat from * until 8 sts remain.

Work row 1 once more. 6 sts.

Cast off all sts.

Repeat with second ear. Weave in ends.

Finishing

Felt by tossing the monkey into the washing machine with a pair of old jeans. Run it on a warm setting, fairly gentle, checking it often. (A hot wash will felt faster, but you'll have less control, and will need to check it a lot more frequently. Washing machines differ, so trust your eyes, and your instincts – you're looking for a fabric that is stiff enough to hold its shape, but not so stiff that the shape becomes distorted. I'd wait until the stitches are blurred almost completely, but not quite. If you're making both pillows, felt them at the same time).

Sew on eyes, nose, and smile as pictured. Stuff very lightly, as we're making pillows, not monkey-shaped balls. Keep it as flat as you can. Sew up opening, and pull the ends through.

Resources

Below are just a few of the many online suppliers of yarns. Most ship internationally.

US

Jimmy Beans Wool
They describe themselves as "your online local yarn store", and their selection is amazing. Most of the yarns in this book are available there

www.jimmybeanswool.com

The Loopy Ewe
This is a good place to go searching for hard-to-find yarns made in smaller batches by very small companies. They carry the usual crowd as well, of course.

www.theloopyewe.com

Yarnmarket
Yarnmarket stocks a wide selection, although it tends toward the higher end of the spectrum. Their Yarn Directory is very useful indeed.

www.yarnmarket.com

WEBS Yarn
They have pretty good discounts, and a decent selection from reasonable to splurge yarns.

http://www.yarn.com

UK

Designer Yarns Ltd
Has details of all the UK and European stockists of Noro, Louisa Harding, Araucania, Debbie Bliss and Mirasol. There is a list of stockists to choose from.

www.designeryarns.uk.com

Loop
Has a shop in Islington, in London; also has an online shop. Stocks a massive selection of brands of wool, as well as patterns and accessories.

www.loopknitting.com

Ball and Needle
Stock a range of yarns and accessories; also has some end-of-line and discounted products.

www.ballandneedle.co.uk

Simply Wool
Stock home spun yarns made in the Orkney Islands as well as well-known brands.

www.simplywool.com

Scarlet Dash
Massive range of wool and haberdashery materials.

www.scarletdash.co.uk

AUSTRALIA

Moseley Park

Homemade wool, made from the sheep on the farm.

www.moseleyparkhome.com

Black Sheep Wool

Stock a variety of yarns, from cheaper brands to high-end. Also supply knitting accessories.

www.blacksheepwool.com.au

The Wool Shack

Stock imported wools from the UK and Europe as well as Australian brands. Also stocks accessories.

www.thewoolshack.com

Yarn Over

Stock a huge range of yarn types and brands. Also stock accessories.

www.yarnover.com.au

Jo Sharp

Luxury yarns in a huge range of colours.

www.josharp.com

EUROPE

Designer Yarns

English website lists European stockists. There is also an affiliated German site.

www.designeryarns.de

Elle Tricote

French supplier of yarns and patterns.

www.elletricote.com

Index

Acknowledgments

Thank you to my wonderfully efficient and understanding editor Judith Hannam, to Kyle Cathie and everyone at Kyle Books, and to hawk-eyed copyeditor Salima Hirani. To photographer Claire Richardson—my knitting has never looked so good—and to Carol Kearns, for her beautiful and instructive drawings.

Thank you to my blog readers. Thank you to *Yarn Forward* magazine for featuring the blog in their December 2010 issue, and to Running Press. Thank you to Patricia's Yarns in Hoboken, New Jersey, and to The Snow Goose in Milton, Massachusetts.

Thank you to Shar Jacobsen, for teaching me how to knit. Thank you to Regina Joskow, and my many other amazing test knitters.

Thank you to my parents, my sisters and my wonderful family.

Thank you to Noah and Hannah for your everlasting patience with the constant "Not now, I'm knitting . . ."

Thank you to Dave for faith, encouragement, willingness to listen to me rant about tension, drape, ease and other nonsense words, and for your maths heroics.